HALL COUNTY
IN WORLD WAR II

IMAGES
of America

HALL COUNTY
IN WORLD WAR II

Glen Kyle

ARCADIA
PUBLISHING

Copyright © 2012 by Glen Kyle
ISBN 978-0-7385-9401-9

Published by Arcadia Publishing
Charleston, South Carolina

Printed in the United States of America

Library of Congress Control Number: 2012941028

For all general information, please contact Arcadia Publishing:
Telephone 843-853-2070
Fax 843-853-0044
E-mail sales@arcadiapublishing.com
For customer service and orders:
Toll-Free 1-888-313-2665

Visit us on the Internet at www.arcadiapublishing.com

This book is dedicated to all those who brought Hall County
through its trials and truly made it a "Land of Promise."

CONTENTS

ACKNOWLEDGMENTS

Many people were involved in breathing life into this book. First must be Jeff Pierce, whose knowledge of Hall County and organizational skills have served the Northeast Georgia History Center and this book well. My appreciation also goes to Ronda Sanders and the Hall County Library for their willingness to share just a few of their wonderful images. Debbie Thompson at the Brenau University Archives was also incredibly helpful in pointing me in the right direction. The staff and volunteers at the Northeast Georgia History Center have been incredibly supportive in this and other projects over the last few years, and our organization is blessed to have such dedicated individuals.

Foremost in my appreciation and love, however, are my wife, Priscilla, and our two sons, Brendan and Andrew, who always inspire, encourage, and give me someone to share stories with.

Unless otherwise noted, all images appear courtesy of the photograph archives at the Northeast Georgia History Center.

INTRODUCTION

World War II was the largest and most significant event in the history of human civilization. No other single circumstance reached to all corners of the globe, affecting nearly every human on the planet in some way or another. Indeed, the war was so pervasive it is difficult to grasp the gigantic global forces at play in the 1930s and 1940s. In small towns all over America, however, life still went on. The war proved to be a turning point not only in world and American history, but in individual communities as well.

Hall County was one of those small, rural communities that was both representative and unique. In the years immediately before the war, the county seat, Gainesville, stood its greatest trial when a tornado nearly destroyed the town. With the city laid waste, its citizens proved stronger than any adversity, and the aftermath of the destruction forged a spirit that grew to define the entire region and prepared citizens of Hall County for the war to come. While this book cannot possibly tell the entire story of Hall County and its people during World War II, it is hoped that it brings about better understanding and appreciation of the years before, during, and after World War II.

A brief introduction will set the stage, telling of the county's importance to the region and of formative events in the 1930s, including the tornado of 1936. The tornado not only had a lasting effect on the spirit of the area, it brought about an intense rebuilding effort that set the stage for Hall County to be the center of policy, communication, and production for the entire northeast Georgia region. This section includes never-before-seen images showing damage from the tornado and the reconstruction as a result of that damage, including significant assistance from the WPA. Other New Deal programs, such as the Civilian Conservation Corps (CCC), helped prepare the area and its young men for the looming world war.

When the war came, Hall County had its first significant military presence with the Gainesville Naval Air Station (NAS) and school for radio and navigation. In addition to the airfield, Hall County had direct contact with the military, as hundreds of young men and women also put on the uniform of their nation. Many of their stories are told in this work, including members of all military branches. For example, Hall Countian John Jacobs served as a forward artillery observer for the 30th Infantry Division as it moved through France, Belgium, Holland, and into Germany. In the course of his service, he was awarded two Silver Stars for heroism under fire and single-handedly captured 25 German soldiers—with only a pistol.

Hall County's home-front efforts defined everyday life for men, women, and children. Sharing part of the national experience in terms of rationing, familial separation, and "making do," the area also had unique aspects owing to its location and geography. Several important industries were located in the county, such as three textile mills, and an examination of these industries and their products will be done with original images and professionally arranged and photographed montages of artifacts. For example, Jesse Jewell, the father of the poultry industry for the entire region, geared up his business and produced enough to be awarded the rare "A" award by the government for excellence and efficiency in production.

Rationing, air-raid drills, scrap and bond drives, and recruiting efforts were daily events in Hall County. A newspaper article and original map give details of Gainesville's efforts in the summer of 1942 to prepare for aerial attack by having a mock "bombing" of the city center, which was complete with casualties, air-defense measures, and firefighting drills. V-mail allowed much faster communication between the home front and the battle front than had ever been possible in previous wars. There are not only several unique and poignant letters in the book, but also one of the dreaded telegrams notifying a loved one that their son had been killed in action.

With the efforts and sacrifices by the "greatest generation," Hall County emerged from the war determined to make the new world a better place. Even before the war had ended, there were plans underway to improve public services and increase business and living opportunities. A new prosperity was illustrated by new construction and new businesses throughout the county. The Jewell Company, mentioned previously, had greatly expanded during the war and had become the largest agricultural business in the entire state. With such success came a need for more workers and more infrastructure, and postwar development that took place in Hall County was akin to a golden age that brought the entire region along with it.

Postwar events and changes meant more than just material prosperity; society had changed for the better as well, especially for women and minorities. Women's experiences during the war had not only shown they were capable of performing "men's work," but it had given them the confidence to take on larger roles. For example, Lessie Smithgall cofounded with her husband the first daily paper in the region, the *Gainesville Times*, which is still in print today. The war brought about new confidences and opportunities for African Americans, and the postwar economic boom not only brought prosperity to traditionally black neighborhoods, but the individual and national experiences also planted the seeds for what would become the Civil Rights movement.

World War II thrust Hall County, as it did much of the South, towards changes and prosperity that would not have been possible in 1940. Social, political, and economic changes accelerate during wartime, creating opportunities not possible in peace. While many recognize this effect on a national scale, this book brings the subject to a more intimate level. To paraphrase Tip O'Neill, "All history is local." Local histories are the building blocks from which larger national events spring, and it is hoped that this book will give the reader a more intimate glimpse into just one of those blocks.

One

HALL COUNTY
BEFORE THE WAR

Hall County was formed in 1826 and named for Lyman Hall, a signer of the Declaration of Independence for Georgia. From its founding, the county would become a central player in the development of the entire northeast Georgia region. During the Civil War, Hall County emerged relatively unscathed, and shortly thereafter the railroad came to Gainesville. Rail transportation changed the county forever, linking it with major cities to the south and making it the central transportation center for the entire region. This meant economic, population, and material growth for the county and all its surrounding areas. By the 1930s, Hall County was the center of commerce and transportation for the entire northeast region of the state and had the largest population as well. Affluence and commercial success meant Gainesville became quite cosmopolitan, with numerous multi-story buildings, factories, and fine homes. During this time, however, Hall County would face two of its greatest challenges: The Depression and the tornado of 1936. The county and its citizens would come through both of these trials ready to face another world war.

Many of the roads in Hall County before the war were rural dirt roads that could be difficult to navigate in bad weather. There were, however, more of them in Hall County than in the rural counties that surrounded it due to the relative urban nature and proximity of Gainesville and the railroad. These dirt roads were arteries in which the produce of farms flowed to the depots to be shipped to other markets.

This photograph shows Christmas on the Gainesville Square at night around 1935. The lights were all part of the festivities, and the entire town would be decorated every year to celebrate the season. Then, as now, it also meant opportunity for the downtown stores to show off their finest wares.

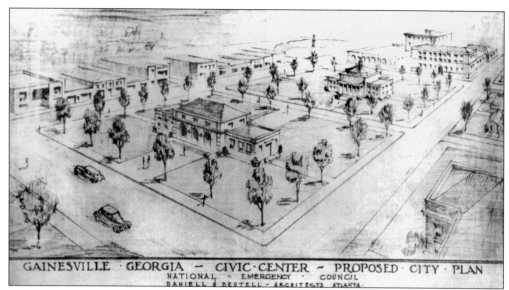

GAINESVILLE · GEORGIA — CIVIC · CENTER — PROPOSED · CITY · PLAN
NATIONAL · EMERGENCY · COUNCIL
DANIELL & BEUTELL · ARCHITECTS · ATLANTA·

After the tornado, city planning became of paramount importance. After the shock of the destruction had passed, the city saw the opportunity to modernize and beautify, and so they did with quite grand arrangements. Plans were developed that shifted the city center from the square to a new three-block area with a courthouse, city hall, and civic center dominating the downtown area. This required money, and so a delegation was sent to Washington, DC, to secure funds from FDR's New Deal administration. They were successful, and construction began immediately. (Below, courtesy Hall County Library.)

These three Gainesville High cheerleaders were typical of local students eager to support their school. The high school was only a block away from the square in the 1930s and was thus closely tied to the community. As with most southern towns, sports played an important role. (Courtesy Hall County Library.)

The Downey Hospital was constructed in 1912 and was the first permanent medical institution in Hall County. Begun by Dr. Philip Downey, its presence on Sycamore Street was a sign of Gainesville's growth and "modern" status, as it had a functional, 24-hour hospital. Dr. Downey and his staff lived on-site. (Courtesy Hall County Library.)

THE PUBLIC IS INVITED TO OUR

Open House

WEEK APRIL 28, THROUGH MAY 3, 1941

NATIONAL

CHILD HEALTH WEEK

Dedicated To

NATIONAL DEFENSE

See The Exhibits on Two of the GREATEST
Problems Facing Our Defense Program

VENEREAL DISEASE
and
MALNUTRITION

You Can Learn How To "Do Your Bit To
Keep Them Fit" By Attending This Exhibit

At The

Hall County
Department of Public Health

Corner E. Washington and Sycamore Streets

ALL WEEK STARTING MONDAY, APRIL 28

—America's Health Is America's Strength—

Even before the war came to America, citizens knew that great dangers lay ahead. To increase awareness and prepare for future defense, programs like this one were hosted around the country to address the issues of national defense. Health was a major concern due to the widespread malnutrition that had occurred during the Depression, especially among youth.

On the morning of April 6, 1936, the fifth deadliest tornado in US history ripped through downtown Gainesville, killing 203 people, injuring 1,500, and causing well over $15 million in damages. This photograph shows the town square only two days later. This deadly event, while tragic, became one of the most defining moments in the history of Gainesville. Though it took years to rebuild, the experience made the community stronger and prepared it in many ways for the war to come.

Brenau College did not escape destruction, as shown by this image of Pierce Auditorium taken two days after the storm. The damage here is a result of a third tornado spawned by the two that had struck Gainesville's square. Though there was significant damage, Brenau began holding classes again only a few days later.

Debris and parts of buildings blocked every road in downtown Gainesville, including Main Street, shown here. Entire structures had completely collapsed. As can be seen in this photograph, most roads in the downtown area were totally impassible, as were many of the roads heading out of town. Because the streets were closed and since most phone lines had been cut, it took the outside world several hours to learn of the destruction in Gainesville.

The great loss of life meant significant changes for many families. Here, a volunteer with the National Youth Administration, a New Deal program, provides care for children whose parents were injured or killed by the tornado.

This photograph was taken from the top of the Jackson Building a day after the tornado and shows the extent of destruction. In the background on the left is the train depot, and next to it is the Cooper Pants Factory, where the greatest loss of life occurred. "Old Joe," the memorial statue to Confederate Soldiers, somehow survived.

This is an image taken from the same spot a few weeks after the tornado. Most of the rubble has been removed, roads have been cleared, and as can be seen from the signs businesses have even managed to reopen. This was to ensure their own survival but also as a service for citizens so they could get what they needed to live.

Many New Deal programs were used to help Gainesville rebuild. Here, the Works Progress Administration provides labor and assistance with the rebuilding of a downtown business. An almost totally rebuilt business and residential district meant that Gainesville would be in an excellent economic position when the war came.

Some buildings could not be repaired and thus were totally rebuilt. Pictured is a store being rebuilt from the ground up using the original foundation. Again, the WPA provided most of the federal money that went to rebuilding the downtown area.

By the fall of 1938, Gainesville had been cleared of most of the rubble. In this photograph, rebuilding has proceeded at a great pace. In the upper right, the completed courthouse is visible, and in front of it the foundation of city hall is being prepared.

The Hall County Courthouse, made of limestone quarried nearby, was built with modern design but also with an eye towards being strong enough to survive any further natural disasters. The fact that it still stands today—looking almost new—is testimony to the skill with which it was created.

Official Program

Roosevelt Squares Dedication

Thanksgiving Day, November 25, 1937
Gainesville, Georgia
Postponed Until March 23, 1938

A program was distributed to all attendees of the dedication of Roosevelt Square. Notice that it had originally been scheduled for November 1937, but due to construction delays as well as President Roosevelt's schedule, it was postponed until the following spring. Rather than reprint the entire program, the new date was simply stamped on the front.

In March 1938, after construction of the new downtown area was complete, President Roosevelt visited Gainesville to help dedicate the new square, which was named for him in appreciation of the role he played in securing funds for the citizens of Gainesville in their hour of need. Here, the speaker's stand has been set up in front of the new city hall. It was one of the largest gatherings the town had ever seen, and it was the first time that a sitting president had visited.

President Roosevelt spoke for only a few minutes, but his speech was well received. He spoke from a podium that had been custom built specifically for his visit, and that podium became one of Hall County's most treasured possessions. It was used for all-important events from that time on—and still is. It currently resides at Gainesville High School.

Two

The Home Front

News of the attack on Pearl Harbor shocked everyone in Hall County, much as it did around the world. With it came a determination to see the war through to its bitter end. As it began, so did the sacrifices. Most difficult to endure, though, were loved ones leaving home to an unknown fate; fathers, sons, brothers, and sometimes even daughters and sisters were needed for the massive war effort. Those remaining on the home front would do their part as well. Preparations were made for civil defense, scrap drives, bond drives, and efforts to get the fighting men what they needed. Rationing took effect and limited the availability of almost every type of supply that folks had taken for granted before the war, such as food, gas, clothing, shoes, and even candy bars. Through it all, those in Hall County exhibited a "can-do" spirit that reflected their inner strength, born of the destruction and rebirth from disaster the decade before.

In the weeks and months after Pearl Harbor, patriotic fervor meant that volunteer enlistments occurred in great numbers. This recruiting ad not only encourages enlistment, it offers additional enticements that would not be available to draftees.

A selective-service card in the mail meant that the addressee had been called up for service. Though volunteerism was strong, two thirds of men who served in the military during World War II did so as draftees. It is important to remember, though, that such service did not carry with it the stigma developed later during the Vietnam War. The vast majority of drafted servicemen were willing to serve their country to fight against fascism.

With so many young men entering military service, civil defense and home-guard units made up of men too old to serve in the regular military sprung up around the nation, and Gainesville was no different. Here is Gainesville's Company A, 2nd Battalion of the Georgia State Guard formed up for inspection in front of the high school. In front is Capt. J. Larry Kleckly, commander of the company. Note the podium used by President Roosevelt during his visit in 1936.

The war touched everyone, especially children who were trying to grow up in difficult times. Above is the "Guard of Green Street Place," a group of children who formed a militia unit to protect their street from enemy attack. Their "commander," Happy Kirkpatrick, asked her father to arm the crew with their handmade wooden rifles before he went off to serve as a doctor with the US Army in the Pacific. The unidentified boy to the left is wearing a typical patriotic uniform very popular throughout the period. The outfits could be purchased from stores or through the mail or were made by mothers at home.

Children have always used playtime and dress-up to deal with the world around them, and wartime was no different. Martial costumes were very popular for boys and girls, and as rationing and availability allowed, they were snatched up. This rather complete outfit reflects actual military dress uniforms and is possibly a based on those used at Riverside Military Academy in Gainesville.

Rosanna Pilcher, a Gainesville native, went to Brunswick, Georgia, with her husband to work at the J.A. Jones Shipyard. J.A. Jones constructed over 85 Liberty Ships. As ships were launched, there was usually a ceremony, and Pilcher was chosen to sing at several of them. Here, she is singing at the launching of the USS *Whitehead* in 1943. Usually, she sang "God Bless America," but for some reason the bandmaster decided to go with "Beautiful Dreamer" on this particular occasion.

The USS *Whitehead* was launched from the Brunswick Shipyards after a proper ceremony. The Liberty Ships were designed so they could be built quickly and cheaply and were a major factor in American victory. Each vessel could carry over 9,000 tons of cargo in its hold plus larger equipment, such as airplanes and tanks, lashed to its upper deck. Since the United States was separated from each theater of conflict by a vast ocean, these ships became crucial in moving the product of America's war machine overseas.

Son-in-service banners were displayed in windows to signify that someone from that home was serving in the military. This one hanging in the window of Anne Fultz of Murrayville shows that four of her loved ones were in service. A silver star over the blue meant that they were serving overseas. A gold star indicated that the loved one had died in service, but fortunately Anne Fultz's banner had none of those.

Larger businesses or groups would have banners to indicate that members or loved ones were in service, and the larger the banner, the larger the group. In this case, an extended family has created a banner for a family reunion to indicate relatives in military service. Notice the scarcity of men of military age in the photograph.

Not all women who contributed to the war effort were "Rosie the Riveter" factory workers. For those who were called into the factories, concerns for child care arose. From left to right, Mildred Right, Jean Ward, Kitty Springle, Fanny DeLong, Hilda Walker, and Carolyn Hartley pose with the children they watched on a daily basis.

Other efforts by women could be small yet incredibly meaningful to men at the front. This group of women met regularly to knit and sew items to send to servicemen, including hats, scarves, ditty bags, and even full sweaters.

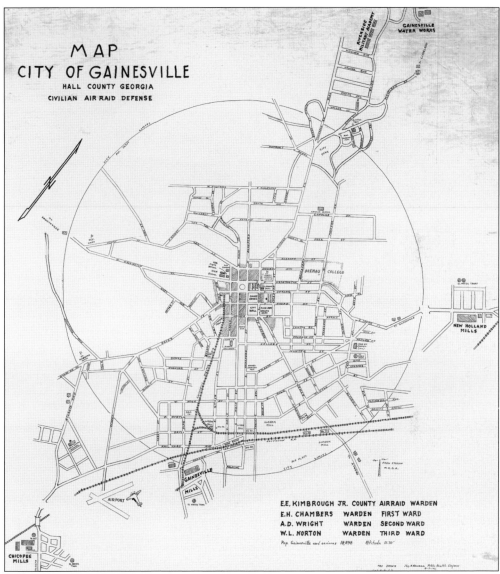

MAP
CITY OF GAINESVILLE
HALL COUNTY GEORGIA
CIVILIAN AIR RAID DEFENSE

E.E. KIMBROUGH JR. COUNTY AIRRAID WARDEN
E.H. CHAMBERS   WARDEN   FIRST WARD
A.D. WRIGHT   WARDEN   SECOND WARD
W.L. NORTON   WARDEN   THIRD WARD

Civil defense and preparation for air raids were of great concern, especially in the early days of the war. This map was created by the Civil Defense Council to help Gainesville residents with their tasks. On May 24, 1942 (only six months after Pearl Harbor), the city held a mock air raid, complete with bomb disposal, rescues from "burning" buildings, and casualty transport to Downey Hospital. This was done to demonstrate preparedness to the civilian population as much as for practice.

Carolyn Westmoreland had two sons in the Army. These envelopes from letters they wrote to her gave some idea as to a mother's worry for her children. One son was stationed in the Pacific with a fighter squadron battling the Japanese, and another was in Europe with a tank destroyer battalion fighting the Germans. The mere arrival of such letters with words that the senders were in good health could bring joy the likes of which most people are unfamiliar with today.

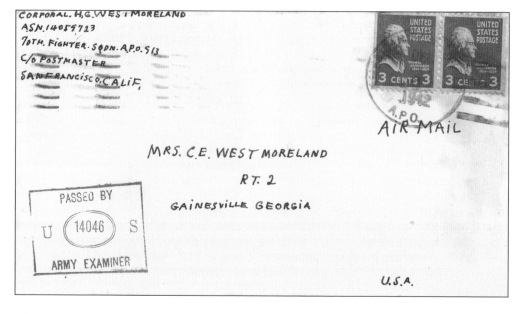

Bond drives to raise money for the war effort were an ever-present part of the American home front. In total, 85 million Americans purchased bonds totaling approximately $185.7 billion, enough to fund nearly two thirds of the total cost of the war. Sgt. Victor Emanuel, a wounded frontline veteran, speaks on the square in Gainesville to encourage people to buy war bonds.

Owen Osbourne was a Gainesville business that made, among other things, silk stockings before the war. Geared up for war production during a bond drive, it offered a special incentive where a donor's name could be placed on a bomb that would actually be dropped on the enemy. Promotions like this were quite popular.

This is the children's Sunday school class at the First Baptist Church. In times of war, communities depended upon their churches a great deal for council, support, and spiritual guidance. They often provided more tangible contributions as well: the First Baptist Church contributed over $5,000 in war bonds during the war.

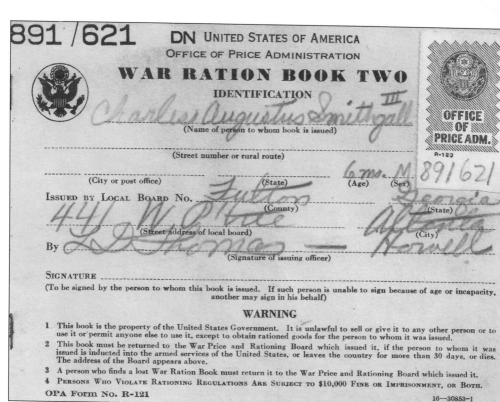

891 /621

DN UNITED STATES OF AMERICA
OFFICE OF PRICE ADMINISTRATION

WAR RATION BOOK TWO

IDENTIFICATION

Charles Augustus Smithgall III

(Name of person to whom book is issued)

_____
(Street number or rural route)

_____   _____
(City or post office)   (State)   6 mo. M   891 621
                                            (Age) (Sex)

ISSUED BY LOCAL BOARD NO. *Fulton* *Georgia*
                                    (County)   (State)

44 W. Pike *Atlanta*
(Street address of local board)   (City)

By *L.D. Thomas* — *Howell*
        (Signature of issuing officer)

SIGNATURE _____
(To be signed by the person to whom this book is issued. If such person is unable to sign because of age or incapacity, another may sign in his behalf)

OFFICE OF PRICE ADM.
R-123

WARNING

1 This book is the property of the United States Government. It is unlawful to sell or give it to any other person or to use it or permit anyone else to use it, except to obtain rationed goods for the person to whom it was issued.
2 This book must be returned to the War Price and Rationing Board which issued it, if the person to whom it was issued is inducted into the armed services of the United States, or leaves the country for more than 30 days, or dies. The address of the Board appears above.
3 A person who finds a lost War Ration Book must return it to the War Price and Rationing Board which issued it.
4 PERSONS WHO VIOLATE RATIONING REGULATIONS ARE SUBJECT TO $10,000 FINE OR IMPRISONMENT, OR BOTH.

OPA Form No. R-121

16—30853-1

Ration books were one of the most common sights in wartime, reminding citizens that there was a war and they could contribute in meaningful ways. For the duration of World War II, each person in each family received a book of coupons that could be used to purchase necessities. Both the coupons and money were required, and items could not be purchased unless both were available. This book belonged to Charles Smithgall, who lived in Atlanta during the war.

With processed foods being rationed, backyard gardens (called Victory Gardens) became very popular. There were entire industries built around their upkeep and maintenance, and to preserve the food that was grown home canning became an important part of the home-front kitchen.

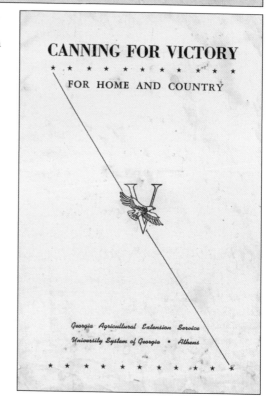

CANNING FOR VICTORY

★ ★ ★ ★ ★ ★ ★ ★ ★ ★ ★ ★ ★

FOR HOME AND COUNTRY

Georgia Agricultural Extension Service
University System of Georgia • Athens

★ ★ ★ ★ ★ ★ ★ ★ ★ ★ ★ ★ ★

A BASIC MILEAGE RATION

UNITED STATES OF AMERICA
OFFICE OF PRICE ADMINISTRATION

R 0129107

IMPORTANT INSTRUCTIONS

1. Coupons can be used only in connection with the vehicle described on the front cover. Detached coupons are VOID.

2. If you stop using your car, this book and all unused coupons must be surrendered to your Board within 5 days.

3. If you sell your car, this book and all unused coupons must be surrendered to your Board. The purchaser will not be issued a gasoline ration unless he presents the receipt which you receive at the time of such surrender.

☆ GPO

NAME OF REGISTERED OWNER *Chas A Smithgall*

ADDRESS—NUMBER AND STREET

CITY AND STATE

LICENSE No. AND STATE *E 108 79* YEAR MODEL AND MAKE *'39 — Packard*

Holder must fill in any blank spaces above before the first purchase of gasoline.

Gasoline and fuel oil were two of the most highly rationed items, as they were obviously crucial to the war effort in a modern mechanized conflict. The "A" card above, the most commonly issued, limited the holder to only four gallons per week. Certain professions, such as doctors or positions important to the war effort, received more. The fuel oil card below was of less concern in Hall County as in other places due to the relatively mild winters, but careful use was still necessary.

Form OPA R-1107

UNITED STATES OF AMERICA
OFFICE OF PRICE ADMINISTRATION
V - FUEL OIL RATION
Class 3 Consumer Coupons
(One-Gallon Coupons)

This Coupon Sheet ~~Not~~ Valid   R.B.

Copy this number in ink on each coupon in the space provided. After each 5 or 10 entries, check against original number for accuracy.

V 592717 AC7

Date issued .... 194... Date expires ...., 194...

These coupons are issued to ....

(Number and street or R. F. D.) (City or post office)

(County) (State)

and consists of .... coupons of 1 gallon each, a total of .... gallons.

Dealers in fuel oil or their representatives are hereby authorized to deliver fuel oil to the above person or his agent for use at the above address, and are required to detach from this sheet coupons having a gallonage value equal to the quantity of oil delivered, in accordance with the rules and regulations of the Office of Price Administration in effect at the time of such delivery. At the time of delivery, the dealer or his agent must fill in the delivery record below.

War Price and Rationing Board No. .... at ....

(County) (City) (State)

By ....

Received by ....

COUPONS VOID IF DETACHED

Permits Delivery of 1 GALLON FUEL OIL OFFICE OF PRICE ADM. No.

34

Not only was gasoline rationed, but all production of civilian automobiles ceased as America's industry geared up to produce war materiel. Nevertheless, the need for vehicles and the items to keep them running was still significant. Here is a bill of sale for a 1942 Ford (from the last run) showing that the price of the car was $1,575, not an insignificant sum.

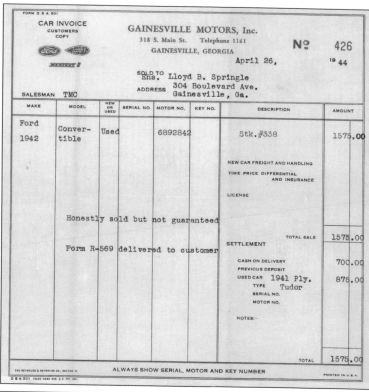

FORM D S A 501

CAR INVOICE
CUSTOMERS COPY

GAINESVILLE MOTORS, Inc.
318 S. Main St. Telephone 1161
GAINESVILLE, GEORGIA

Nº 426

April 26, 19 44

SOLD TO
Ens.' Lloyd B. Springle
ADDRESS 304 Boulevard Ave.
Gainesville, Ga.

SALESMAN TMC

MAKE	MODEL	NEW OR USED	SERIAL NO.	MOTOR NO.	KEY NO.	DESCRIPTION	AMOUNT
Ford 1942	Convertible	Used		6892842		Stk.#338	1575.00
						NEW CAR FREIGHT AND HANDLING	
						TIME PRICE DIFFERENTIAL AND INSURANCE	
						LICENSE	
						Honestly sold but not guaranteed	
						Form R-569 delivered to customer	
						TOTAL SALE	1575.00
						SETTLEMENT	
						CASH ON DELIVERY	700.00
						PREVIOUS DEPOSIT	
						USED CAR 1941 Ply.	875.00
						TYPE Tudor	
						SERIAL NO.	
						MOTOR NO.	
						NOTES:-	
						TOTAL	1575.00

THE REYNOLDS & REYNOLDS CO., DAYTON, O.
D S A 501

ALWAYS SHOW SERIAL, MOTOR AND KEY NUMBER

PRINTED IN U.S.A.

O. P. A. FORM R-704

THIS CERTIFICATE MAY NOT BE REPRODUCED.

UNITED STATES OF AMERICA

OFFICE OF PRICE ADMINISTRATION

PART C

(TWO MEMBERS OF THE BOARD, AND THE PERSON TO WHOM THE CERTIFICATE IS ISSUED MUST SIGN AT THE PLACES INDICATED.)

CERTIFICATE SERIAL NO.
90144 -B
DATE OF ISSUE

(1)

IDENTIFICATION

(TO BE RETAINED BY PERSON AUTHORIZED TO ACQUIRE NEW ADULT BICYCLES)

(THIS PORTION TO BE FILLED IN BY WAR PRICE AND RATIONING BOARD)

(2) 43-37-1
(BOARD NUMBER)

(3) (PERSON TO WHOM CERTIFICATE IS ISSUED)
Alford Catherine Y
(LAST NAME) (FIRST NAME) (MIDDLE INITIAL)

125 E Washington St.
(R. F. D. OR STREET & NUMBER)

304 Boulevard St.
(R. F. D. OR STREET & NUMBER)

Gainesville Hall Ga.
(CITY, COUNTY & STATE)

Gainesville Hall Ga.
(CITY OR POSTOFFICE, COUNTY & STATE)

(4) OCCUPATION OR WORK FOR WHICH BICYCLE IS TO BE USED:
(A) GAINFUL OCCUPATION OR BUSINESS To go to and from work at the Alford lumber Co.
(B) VOLUNTARY WORK

CERTIFICATION

THIS IS TO CERTIFY THAT THE ABOVE-MENTIONED PERSON HAS BEEN AUTHORIZED TO ACQUIRE

One NEW ADULT BICYCLE(S) FOR Use BY PART "A" OF THIS CERTIFICATE.
(WRITE OUT NUMBER) (USE OR SALVAGE)

(5) (SIGNATURE OF PERSON TO WHOM CERTIFICATE IS ISSUED. MUST BE SIGNED IN PRESENCE OF MEMBER OR CLERK OF BOARD)

(6) (SIGNATURE OF MEMBER OF BOARD)

(7) (SIGNATURE OF MEMBER OF BOARD)

(THIS PORTION TO BE FILLED IN BY TRANSFEROR)

(8) (NAME OF TRANSFEROR)

229 Main St
(R. F. D. OR STREET & NUMBER)

Gainesville Hall Ga.
(CITY OR POSTOFFICE, COUNTY & STATE)

(21) DESCRIPTION OF NEW ADULT BICYCLES DELIVERED

DELIVERY DATE	MAKE AND MODEL	FRAME SIZE	SERIAL NUMBER	PRICE PAID
7-14-43	Girls Mercury	26"	MG 1164	33.50

(IF ADDITIONAL SPACE IS NEEDED, USE SEPARATE SHEET AND ATTACH FIRMLY HERETO)

When cars were not available due to tire or rubber rationing, bicycles became the most popular means of local transportation. Demand grew so high, though, that even this commodity came to be rationed. Here is a certificate granting permission for Catherine Alford to purchase a bicycle, something that would have to be presented to the salesman before he could make the sale.

One of three mills in the county, Gainesville Mill produced cotton fabric for the war effort. Millwork, a primary industry in Hall County before the war, was one of the region and state's most significant contributions to the war effort. (Courtesy of Hall County Library.)

Like most mill villages, the relationship between employer and employee could be one of significant dependence. Housing, food, clothing, and even leisure and worship could be provided for the workers by the company. Below is the general store on the site of Gainesville Mill, where most necessities could be purchased on credit against future earnings. Such a situation often led to significant indebtedness on the part of the workers.

Jesse Jewell was a man with a vision who, in the postwar years, made Gainesville the center of a vast agricultural business. His efforts at improving and growing the poultry industry began to take root during World War II when his company provided poultry foods to the military. So successful was his company that it was awarded the prestigious "A" award for excellence in agricultural production. Below is the cover of the program for the award ceremony held at Jewell's poultry production facility.

Presentation
OF THE
WAR FOOD ADMINISTRATION
ACHIEVEMENT "A" AWARD
TO THE MEN AND WOMEN OF
J. D. JEWELL
GAINESVILLE, GA.

FOR OUTSTANDING PRODUCTION
IN FOOD PROCESSING

Today, Gainesville is known as the "Poultry Capital of the World," and it got that title thanks largely to one man, Jesse Jewell, who made his mark during the war with his food production for the military. Here, Jewell (far right of the flag, holding its corner) is receiving the prestigious "A" award from the Department of Agriculture. He was awarded for excellence and efficiency in wartime production.

CHICOPEE MFG. CORP. OF GEORGIA		
W-E-2-13-43		
156		
258-09-9314		
HOWARD H. KENNEY		
Insurance	44	
Rent		
Stove		
Medical		
Loan	3	67
WAR BONDS		
VICTORY TAX	9	0
Federal Old Age Tax	2	9
GROSS WAGES	29	44
LESS : DEDUCTIONS	5	30
NET AMOUNT	24	14
Received		

Retain This Statement. . . . It Is Your Social Security Record

Chicopee Mills was another major textile industry in Hall County. In the photograph above, the plant as well as the mill village can be seen; it shows how a small, self-sufficient community could be created and nurtured with a dependent work force nearby. The communities at these mills became very close and were practically towns in their own right. At left is a pay envelope for Howard Kenney.

New Holland Mills, the fourth of the larger southern company Pacolet, was Hall County's oldest textile mill. Like the other two, it provided cotton goods to the military. Part of its village can be seen in this image. Note the proximity of the rail line, a necessity for rapid transport of raw materials and goods to and from the mill.

Here is another view of New Holland's mill village. This postcard image illustrates the uniformity and proximity of mill housing. Housing was built and furnished by the company, and withholdings from workers' paychecks were put towards rent.

Pictured are children from the New Holland day-care facility. As mentioned earlier, the mill offered everything its workers could need, and this extended to childcare. It became even more important as the needs of war often meant that either both parents were working or the man of the house had been called to military service, leaving the wife as the only breadwinner of the family. (Courtesy Hall County Library.)

Three

GAINESVILLE NAVAL AIR STATION

Gainesville leaders, among them Edgar Dunlap, used their influence to make sure that Hall County would not be left out of the incredible growth that the US military was creating around the country. A few years prior, a small dirt airstrip had been built just outside of town, and as the war was coming to a close it was decided that the Navy would build an auxiliary airstrip there to serve the naval air station also being built in Atlanta. Accompanying this naval air station would be a Naval school that would teach radio navigation and ground-controlled approach, some of the most advanced flight methods and technologies available at the time. Two new airstrips were added to the first, and all three were paved. Buildings were constructed to house personnel, equipment, and offices, and soon Hall County had its own military base.

This photograph represents one of the first taken of the prewar landing strip. Aviation was a young and new experience, and these fliers were truly pioneers. (Courtesy Hall County Library.)

An aerial view of the school shows the runways and buildings. It is also evident that the facility was still relatively primitive and that Gainesville, even though it was considered the most "urbanized" area in northeast Georgia, was still a rural town.

The air station is seen at its height of activity during the war. From a single dirt strip with one ramshackle building, it had grown into a large facility housing Naval aircraft and personnel that had numerous flights every day. All of the aircraft in the photograph have military markings, though most are of various types. (Courtesy Hall County Library.)

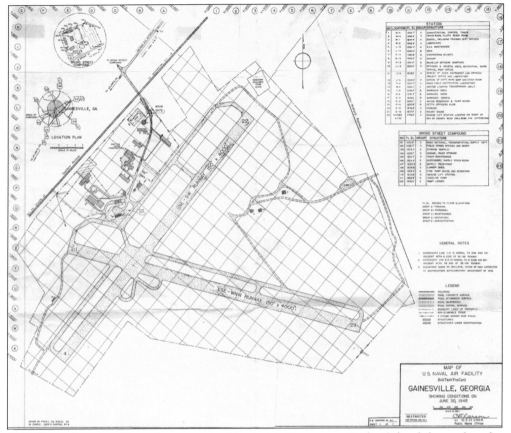

Hall County's only military base was the Naval Air Navigation Radio School, located at the county municipal airport, which was being leased to the government for $1 a year. The base served as a sub-unit of the naval air station in Atlanta and was commissioned on August 20, 1943. The map shown illustrates the significant growth of the facility towards the end of the war, and the photograph below shows an actual image compared to the land plat.

By the end of the war, several buildings had been constructed at the naval air station to accommodate increased operations. The page at right from a wartime promotional brochure for the airfield shows the administration and laboratory building. Unfortunately, the only structure that remains from the war years is the first story of the flight tower. Below is a piece of stationary used by one of the students in the school to work out radio-frequency effectiveness.

Naval Air Navigation Radio School
GAINESVILLE, GEORGIA

The twisted wreckage of a thousand planes on mountain sides, plains and beneath the waters of the seven seas is a sacrifice not entirely in vain. It taught a valuable lesson—a plane that is lost in a fog one mile from its home landing field or a carrier is as lost as if it were a thousand miles away. ★ Here was a challenge—one of the many hundred hurled by this war at American ingenuity. It had to be met quickly and surely in terms of new radio safeguards to pilots and technical men to operate and maintain them. ★ As a part of the Navy's vast system of training personnel for instrument flight work in all its phases, NANRS was established at Gainesville and commissioned 20 August, 1943. ★ There was no time to construct suitable buildings. Training began at once in some barn-like structures then available. Selected classes of students, officers and enlisted men, were put through the course and duly impressed with the importance of the work they would soon be performing, on operating bases and as instructors. Planning and instruction proceeded under the direction of Lieutenant Commander Robert H. Wood, USN, the School's first Officer-in-Charge. Construction of laboratories, classrooms, barracks and other buildings is well under way. ★ With its new plant and larger classes, NANRS may become a separate command.

Left, above: Lieutenant Commander Robert H. Wood, USN, first Officer-in-Charge.
Left, present administration and laboratory building.

NAVAL AIR NAVIGATION RADIO SCHOOL
GAINESVILLE, GA.

IN REPLY REFER TO

No.

Assigned to the Gainesville Naval Air Station, Lt. Lloyd Springle found his future wife, Kitty. She was a native of Gainesville and, like many girls from the area, Kitty found the men in uniform at the air station and school difficult to resist. Married in 1945, after the war Kitty moved with her husband to New England. Below are Lieutenant Springle's officer records from his time in Gainesville.

OFFICER'S QUALIFICATION REPORT	OFFICER QUALIFICATIONS RECORD					

NAVPERS-310C (REV. 9-45)
JACKET COPY

PLEASE TYPE THIS FORM
If no typewriter is available use ink but be sure all copies are legible.   DATE **14 Dec 1945**

1. NAME (last) (first) (middle)	RANK AND CLASSIFICATION	FILE NO.
SPRINGLE Lloyd Bryan	Lt.(jg), USN	304102

SHIP OR STATION
U. S. Naval Air Facility - NATechTraCen, Gainesville, Ga.   PERIOD OF REPORT (mo., day, year) DATE FROM **1 Sept 45** DATE TO **14 Dec 1945**

DATE OF REPORTING TO PRESENT SHIP OR STATION **29 July 1945**   OCCASION FOR REPORT
☐ DETACHMENT OF OFFICER REPORTED ON ☒ DETACHMENT OF REPORTING SENIOR ☐ REGULAR SEMI-ANNUAL ☐ QUARTERLY ☐ SPECIAL

2. DESCRIPTION OF DUTIES SINCE LAST FITNESS REPORT (List most recent first and describe accurately. Include periods of leave, transit, etc., also include employment of ship.)

	FROM MO. YR.	TO MO. YR.
Station Pilot for Instrument Low Approach Project (BuShips) Project 440-44	Sep 45	Dec 4
Member Senior Examining Board	Sept 45	Dec 4
Member Summary Court Martial Board #1	Sept 45	Dec 4

3. Has present duty changed since last fitness report was submitted? ☐ Yes ☒ No
IF COURSES OF INSTRUCTION WERE COMPLETED DURING PERIOD OF THIS REPORT, LIST TITLE OF COURSE, LOCATION OF SCHOOL, LENGTH OF COURSE AND DATE COMPLETED.   Are you physically qualified for Sea Duty? ☒ Yes ☐ No ☐ Don't Know
None

4. If Aviator, indicate No. of Flight Hours Last Two years (List for Each Type Aircraft) (List Most Recent Type First)	TYPE OF AIRCRAFT	RY-1	PBJ	SNB	R4D	R50	SNJ	TOTAL
	NO. OF HOURS	400	100	400	50	200	150	1300

5. MY PREFERENCE FOR NEXT DUTY IS:	SEA	KIND OF DUTY	Transport	LOCATION	No preferenod
	SHORE	KIND OF DUTY	Experimental work	LOCATION	East coast.

6. SECTION 6 TO BE FILLED IN BY REPORTING OFFICER   NAME OF REPORTING OFFICER RANK FILE NO. OFFICIAL STATUS RELATIVE TO OFFICER REPORTED ON
J. T. THORNTON, JR., Comdr., 70276, USN, Commanding Officer

SIGNATURE OF OFFICER REPORTED ON (Applies only to Sections 1 through 5)   SIGNATURE OF REPORTING OFFICER
Lloyd B Springle   *J. T. Thornton Jr.*

When completed remove carbon paper, forward Pages 1 and 2, not detached, to BuPers. Retain Page 3 for "Officer's Qualification Record Jacket".
PAGE 3

48

Another local girl who found love was Mary Whelchel, also of Gainesville. She married Jean M. Morris, and they had their first son while the war was still underway. Like Kitty, Mary followed her husband away from Hall County after the war.

Charles Port, from Owings Mill, Missouri, was one of the sailors stationed at the air station in Gainesville. Pictured is a vehicle used by personnel from the school to ride into Gainesville for entertainment and recreation, and it was certainly not the "latest model." Note the "A" ration sticker in the window, which allowed only four gallons per week to be purchased for this vehicle.

In this photograph, Charles Port (foreground) lounges with friends on the square in Gainesville. Such close proximity to a town with so many young ladies was an advantage not all Navy personnel were lucky enough to experience.

Charles Port, seen above fourth
from the right in the first row with
many of his friends from the naval
air station, spent much time on
the campus of Brenau Women's
College (now Brenau University).
At right is one of Port's friends with
one of the local college girls.

Not limited to Gainesville, Charles Port and his friends found opportunity to travel more widely. These two photographs show a trip to a rural farm in White County after Port had been invited to have a meal with a local family. Such hospitality was very common, heightened by the feeling by those at home that it directly inspired those serving in the military.

Four

GAINESVILLE IN WARTIME

Gainesville, the county seat of Hall County, was the most important city in all of northeast Georgia. In the short time after its founding, it had become a transportation hub for the entire region, and by 1940 it was the most urban area between Atlanta and Charlotte, North Carolina. The major damage caused by the tornado led to a rebuilding that only further enhanced its appearance and contemporary atmosphere. Modern buildings, wares for sale, entertainment, education, and prosperity could be had within city limits. This chapter shows what Gainesville looked like to those who experienced World War II within the boundaries of the city.

Since the tornado of 1936, Gainesville had grown by leaps and bounds. This aerial photograph shows the downtown area in its heyday, with the new government buildings and square as the primary landmarks. (Courtesy Hall County Library.)

Here is an aerial view of Gainesville that shows how the road system radiated out from the town center. Note the extensive growth that has taken place since 1936. (Courtesy Hall County Library.)

Dixie Hunt Hotel
Gainesville, Georgia

In the 1930s, Gainesville's finest establishment was the Dixie Hunt Hotel. Complete with restaurant, barbershop, and a variety of rooms, it was the place where folks wanted to stay when visiting town. This is a view of the hotel before it was damaged by the tornado. (Courtesy Hall County Library.)

In the postcard image above, one can see the refurbished hotel, which was the largest building on the town square. Below is a view of the hotel lobby that customers would see as they entered the building.

The Royal Theatre was the most popular movie house in town. Replete with neon signage and an Art Deco–inspired interior, some of the best motion pictures ever made were shown on its screen. During the war, most people received their news from the newsreels shown before the main feature. (Courtesy of Hall County Library.)

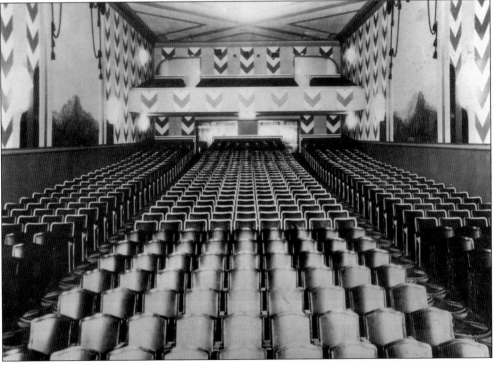

The Ritz was another movie house in Gainesville, though this image shows it decked out to be a Marine Corps recruiting center. The showing of patriotically themed movies could inspire many to volunteer for service, and the Marine Corps and Navy relied totally upon volunteers until 1944. (Courtesy Hall County Library.)

L. and J. Gainesville Theatres

"WHERE HAPPINESS COSTS SO LITTLE"

ROYAL

OPEN SUNDAY

OCTOBER 17, SATURDAY ONLY
Show Starts at 1 P. M. Saturday
"SABOTAGE SQUAD"
Bruce Bennett — Kay Harris
"PACIFIC FRONTIER" — "LIFE WITH FIDO"

OCTOBER 18, SUNDAY MATINEE ONLY
"SWEETHEART OF THE FLEET"
Jinx Falkenburg — Joan Davis — Joan Woodbury
"ARMY NIGHT LIFE"   "SCREEN SNAPSHOTS"

STARTS OCTOBER 19, MON., TUES., WED.
"TALK OF THE TOWN"
Ronald Colman, Cary Grant, Jean Arthur
LATEST METRO NEWS

STARTS OCTOBER 22, THURS., AND FRIDAY
"PIED PIPER"
Monty Woolley   Roddy McDowall
"DONALD'S GARDEN"   "AERO BATTY"   NEWS

Due to increased costs in operation, Adult admissions at the Royal Theatre will be slightly advanced within the coming week.

RITZ A Good Show 11c - 22c - 28c

Starts Oct. 17, Fri. and Satur.
Opens 12 P. M. Saturday
"UNDERGROUND RUSTLER"
Range Busters
"Mail Trouble"
Secret Code No. 4

Starts Oct. 19, Mon. and Tues.
"THIS GUN FOR HIRE"
Veronica Lake — Robert Preston
"Battle of Miday"
Kaltenborn News

STATE House of action 11c-17c-22c

Starts Oct. 17, Fri. and Satur.
"LAND OF OPEN RANGE"
Tim Holt
"Dumbconscious Mind"
"Meet The Champs"
Perils of Nyoka No. 14

Starts Oct. 19, Mon. and Tues.
'MAN FROM HEADQUARTERS'
Frank Albertson—Joan Woodbury
"Electrical Earthquake"
"Salvage"

This newspaper ad shows some of the offerings during the war years. Unlike today, theaters would resurrect older movies and show them for months (and sometimes years) after their release date if they were popular.

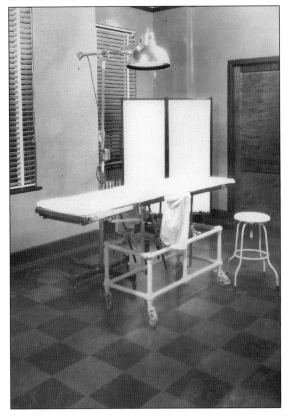

These two photographs give a glimpse into the world of health care in the 1940s. Above is the supervising nurse's office at the Hall County Hospital; at left is the operating room at the same establishment. Most remarkable of all to modern eyes is the total lack of electronics-based technology that patients of the early 21st century have come to identify with health care.

The downtown area was replete with shopping establishments of every kind. Above is the shoe section of a men's clothing store, while below is a storefront display of the latest electrical appliance—the refrigerator. Such items would become rare (in the case of shoes) or nonexistent (in the case of refrigerators) due to national industry tooling up to provide war material rather than consumer goods.

This photograph of the interior of a grocery store on the square in Gainesville is a rare glimpse into shopping in the past. While very different from larger grocery stores of today, there are still many familiar sights and brands, including Kraft Velveeta macaroni and cheese, Cut-Rite aluminum foil, and Ivory soap. Local produce and name brands were available, and even refrigeration of foodstuffs was common as can be seen by the freezer unit in the upper right.

In the 1940s, hardware stores carried household items, kitchenware, and appliances as well as tools, nuts, and bolts. Again, brands familiar today, such as Sherwin Williams and Westinghouse, can be seen. This photograph, like the one on the previous page, is probably a prewar one since availability of new aluminum pots, pans, and foil as well as processed foods would have not been nearly so great as is shown in these displays.

Drugstores, like Whatley's, provided not only pharmaceuticals but also a wide range of items from candy and gum to cameras to small household appliances. They were also very popular "hangouts" for the youth, as they invariably had soda and ice cream stands inside. Whatley's stand is visible just through the door.

A local restaurant, though sparse by current standards, provided good food at decent prices. As the war progressed and rationing took hold, business suffered greatly, as access to certain foodstuffs, especially meats and sugars, made dinner during an outing sometimes more bland than what could be prepared at home.

This prewar image of the federal building in downtown Gainesville shows the classic lines common to such government buildings. Sturdy and strongly built, it survived the tornado with minimal damage, serving no doubt as an example to and model for Gainesville's rebuilt city buildings. This housed the federal courts as well as most other federal groups, including the post office. (Courtesy Hall County Library.)

Gainesville High School, with its gymnasium behind, was right off the square and a central part of the city. Gainesville, already a tight-knit community, was made even closer by the location of its school in the center of town. Miraculously, it survived the tornado even though it was directly in the path of one of the funnel clouds. (Courtesy of Hall County Library.)

Five

EDUCATION IN WARTIME

Brenau College (now a university) and Riverside Academy provided some of the best education available in Georgia. Both formed long before the war came, and the centrality of their position within the community meant that they were not only leading institutions during the war effort, they would contribute leaders to the effort throughout the war.

Founded in 1878 as a women's conservatory, by the 1940s Brenau had become one of the most important signs of Hall County's progress. This photograph shows the center of campus, Yonah Hall, and Pierce Auditorium. Then, as today, it is an iconographic image of Gainesville.

As the United States entered World War II, every aspect of society was mobilized, and the woman's college was no exception. This cover of the 1944 annual reflects the military theme adopted for the entire publication in an effort to show the school's support for the war. Note the nationally ubiquitous "V" symbol of stars.

Postcards were popular wartime souvenirs; this one shows Yonah Hall at Brenau College. Originally this building housed offices and classrooms.

G-23 YONAH HALL FROM SIMMONS BUILDING, BRENAU COLLEGE, GAINESVILLE, GA.

THE ALCHEMIST

Published by Students Union — "REFINED GOLD" — *Brenau College Gainesville, Ga.*

VOLUME XXIX. GAINESVILLE, GEORGIA, TUESDAY, FEBRUARY 16, 1943 Number 7

MARY LOUISE BELTZ PRESENTS RECITAL

NEWS REEL
(Latest World News Summary)

LONDON — The German High Command announces that Russian forces have entered the outer suburbs of Kharkov.

Allied Headquarters, North Africa — An allied headquarters communique announces that small elements of enemy forces have entered Gafsa in Southern Tunisia.

On the Australian front all types of American aircraft—heavy bombers, medium bombers, light bombers, and fighters have been taking part in a widespread offensive against Japanese bases.

In Southern Russia, Soviet columns are driving deeper into the Ukraine and in the Donets basin N. of Rostov. Pushing westward from the Rostov - Moscow railroad, Red Army troops have taken six more towns.

Royal Air Force planes of the India Command have made another series of attacks on Japanese airdromes and other targets in Burma. A daylight bombing attack was made on a village near Akbay, the Japanese-held port on the Bay of Bengal.

Secretary of Agriculture Claude Wickard appears before a Senate Agriculture subcommittee today to discuss the production, transportation and distribution of food. The inquiry covers the American shipments abroad as well as the situation at home.

Dr. Gertrude Brigham

Patricia Mauney Named May Queen
By Frieda Snow

Presiding over the Annual May Day Festival of Brenau on May first will be Miss Patricia Mauney, of Asheville, North Carolina.

Pat is president of Alpha Chi Omega Sorority, Second Vice-president of Student Government, a member of Honor Court and Executive Council, and is in the Senior Y Cabinet.

She will be graduated May 31st, obtaining an A. B. degree with a major in English.

Wylene Pool and Del Goldschmidt were chosen Maid of Honor and Prince Charming respectively.

Patricia Mauney

Dr. G. R. Brigham National President Of Alpha Delta
By Peggy Victor

For the duration national headquarters of Alpha Delta, national honorary journalistic fraternity, will be Brenau College, with Dr. G. R. Brigham as national president pro tem, and Miss Helen Estes, formal national president of Brenau Alumnae, as national secretary pro tem.

All chapters of Alpha Delta scattered throughout many states, have unanimously concurred in this selection of Brenau College. The reason is explained by the President, Max Clowes, of Davenport, Iowa, in a letter to other chapters:

"The effects of the war have already been sorely felt in the National Council of Alpha Delta by the entry of Mr. Dailey, our national Secretary, into the Armed Services. Other officers will shortly be called. . . . It is our proposal that Dr. G. R. Brigham, National Vice-President of Alpha Delta and for many years an ardent worker in the interests of the Fraternity from her post at Brenau College in Gainesville, Ga., be elevated to National President, Pro Tem."

Membership in Alpha Delta is dependent on recommendation of Chapter members, endorsed by the National Officers, and is conferred only for outstanding work in Journalism and on the Brenau publications, Alchemist, Flame and Bubbles, with a high average in other subjects.

Physical Ed Club Presents Yearly Project At Gym

This year the Physical Education Club searched diligently for a worthwhile project that we all might enjoy. After much consideration it was decided to get covers for the mats in the gym.

The girls who have had the opportunity to use them seem much pleased and we hope that you too, will enjoy using them.

Mary Ridgway Is Head Of New Art Club At Brenau

Mary Ridgway, Mary Elizabeth Cawthon, and Betty Rosenbush were named February 4th, as charter members of the Brenau Art Club.

To be eligible for membership one must have a year of art training and a marked artistic ability. Besides a definite interest in art, a C average in all other scholastic work is required.

Mrs. Porter, faculty adviser of the Art Club and head of the Art Department, announced the following new members: Mary Ridgway, president; Mary Elizabeth Cawthon, vice-president; Betty Rosenbush, treasurer; and Alice Richards, Judy Hines, Annette Willke, and Neechie Felder.

Mary Ridgway

BRENAU PROGRAMS TO BE HEARD OVER WGGA

Feb. 16—8:30. Mme Vicarino, Voice Recital.

Feb. 19—8:30. Spanish under direction of Miss Taylor.

Feb. 23—8:30. Mme Ringo, Voice Recital.

Feb. 26—8:30. Mr. Zachara, Piano Recital.

Mr. Kimbrough, head of the Radio Department, has requested that anyone having suggestions to offer as to possible future programs over WGGA will please see him at their earliest convenience.

Famous Contralto Presented In Program Monday Night
EXCEPTIONAL PERFORMANCE WITNESSED

Miss Mary Louise Beltz was presented in the Brenau Auditorium last night, Monday, Feb. 15, at 8:15 P. M. by the Gainesville Federated Music Club, of which Mme. Margeurite Ringo is President. This is the third and last number of the Artist Series sponsored by the club this winter.

Miss Beltz, gifted contralto, is indeed a versatile musician. She is an excellent piano accompanist and plays the harp with equal skill. This exceptional musical knowledge gives her an added advantage in timing when singing with an orchestra.

Miss Beltz is a member of Mu Phi Epsilon, National Honor Music Society, and of Pi Kappa Lambda, Honorary Music Fraternity. She has appeared with the Cleveland Orchestra, with the National Symphony Orchestra in Washington, with the Bach Circle Orchestra in New York, and with the Brico Symphony Orchestra in Carnegie Hall in New York.

Since she was a small girl Mary Louise Beltz has paid careful attention to diction in her singing. She sings in French, German and English with equal fluency.

This attractive and talented young contralto won the coveted National Federation of Music Clubs prize at its Biennial Convention of 1941. She had her early training singing in a church—under the direction of her father, who was minister.

Miss Beltz was offered a scholarship with Irene Peabody and graduated from Kansas University. She holds a Bachelor of Music Degree with the University of Kansas and a Fellowship at Juilliard. Her richness of tone and pureness of diction, as well as her dramatic interpretation makes her program one well worth listening to.

Mary Louise Beltz, Contralto

Marilyn Levinson Is Elected As New Freshman Leader
By Betty Gilkeson

We are all very sorry that Marilyn Levinson wasn't in Chapel last Tuesday, because it was announced then that she was the third and last Freshman Chairman. Marilyn is still in the hospital but she is getting better and we hope she will be out soon.

Upon quizzing Lynette, Marilyn's room-mate, to find out more about her, we find she is from Dayton, Ohio. She graduated from High school there. Her main interest in college is Journalism. The things she writes are very humorous. We might add that her main interest outside of college is Marvin—the Army Air Corps, you know.

Lynn says that anytime anyone is in the dumps, just come around to 91 East and Marilyn will snap them out of it right away. She has a wonderful sense of humor.

As everyone knows—at least the sophomores do anyhow—she is a wonderful sport. She won honorable mention during Rat Week for being such a good sport.

Lynn added that Marilyn is a perfect room-mate, for she has at last found some one who wears the same size clothes that she does. Of course it is a fifty-fifty proposition.

Here's to you, Marilyn! We need more girls like you around.

Marilyn Levinson

The February 1943 issue of the Brenau school paper, the *Alchemist*, shows the level of dedication the school made towards doing its part. At each corner are exhortations to participate in bond drives, of which there were many on campus during the course of the war. There is also "news from the front" from places as far away as Kharkov. This paper represents, in a small way, the newfound equality women were finding through their efforts to participate in national defense.

School- and community-wide efforts were made by Brenau students to contribute to the war effort, and shown here are two instances. The Brenau War Board was formed to coordinate campus activities. Above is a bond-drive booth placed on campus, and below is a joint effort between Brenau and the Navy School to show the role that women were playing in the American military.

Cooperation between Brenau and other local schools took place before as well as during the war. Shown here is the Brenau and Riverside student choir, which performed at various patriotic rallies.

This postcard of Riverside Military Academy shows the front of the main buildings. Chartered in 1906, it began accepting students in 1908. Its purpose was to prepare boys in grades 7 through 12 for the service academies or for a military vocation, but such aspirations were not required to participate in the program.

Riverside Academy, which got its name from the proximity to the banks of the Chattahoochee River, continued to grow. In 1932, its commandant, Col. Sandy Beaver, acquired another campus in Hollywood, Florida, with the intention of having students split the school year between the two. This view is of the Gainesville campus during the war. At the same time, the Florida campus had been leased by the US Navy to use as a housing and training ground for its recruits.

The school's wide area, coupled with its proximity to rural forested areas, meant that plenty of training opportunities were available. Above, students familiarize themselves with machine guns, though these are outdated World War I types. Below, the extent of the main campus and the Chattahoochee River in the foreground can be seen.

Here, the cadets march in review in 1944. Like the service academies and other military institutions around the country, Riverside took its formal occasions and appearances seriously. The cadet body is in full dress regalia, complete with a band. In this instance, they are being reviewed by commissioned officers of the US Army.

Gen. Jonathan Wainwright was left in command of US forces in the Philippines after Douglas MacArthur left in 1942. He was a prisoner of the Japanese until liberated by the Soviets in 1945. Shortly after he returned to the United States, he attended a review of the cadets at Riverside. He can be seen here in a car (back right) with Edgar Dunlap (back left) arriving at the campus.

General Wainwright reviewed the entire student body at Riverside before being honored by the town. He is accompanied by his aide-de-camp as well as by Riverside students. The memory of the embarrassment for Americans at the Battle of Corregidor was assuaged by the presence of the hero Wainwright, and he was later awarded the Medal of Honor.

Six

THOSE WHO FOUGHT

This chapter looks at just a few of the hundreds of men and women from Hall County who served in the armed forces. These brave souls, mostly volunteers, agreed to serve their country in whatever capacity they best could. Called by some the "greatest generation," they grew up during the Depression, lived through the tornado, and were now called to fight in a war that, at the time, no one knew how long would last. The spirit of those who fought, though, meant that there was never any question as to whom would be the victor.

EAGLE PRESENTS ITS "V FOR VICT ORY" FOR 35th CONSECUTIVE WEEK

The Oldest Newspaper
The Largest Weekly
of Northeast Georgia

THE GAINESVILLE EAGLE

The Gainesville Eagle
Is Official Organ
For Hall County

VOLUME LXXXIII. Established 1860 GAINESVILLE, GEORGIA, THURSDAY, AUGUST 5, 1943 83 Years Old NUMBER 2

Camp and Hospital Red Cross Council Is Organized Here

Organization has been perfected here of a camp and hospital council of the American Red Cross, in keeping with a program which is being carried on throughout the country.

Harry Purvis is chairman of the council, and other officers include Mrs. L. F. Quinlan, co-chairman; R. M. Mathews, of the Lions club; O. J. Lilly, of Kiwanis; J. D. Jewell of the Elks; Mrs. John W. Jackson, on committee at large.

Function of the camp and hospital council is to supplement services of the Army and Navy and of the Red Cross, and assist in meeting this responsibility where the military does not reach. There is no solicitation of funds except as specific council needs

—Continued on Editorial Page

In Florida

Private First Class Alvin Elrod, son of Mr. and Mrs. Melvin Elrod of Murrayville, who enlisted in the U. S. Air forces last December after completing an N.Y.A. course at Clarkesville. He received his basic training at Miami Beach, Fla., and is now with a guard squadron stationed at the airbase in Miami. His wife, the former Miss Ruby Robinson of this city, also lives in Miami.

Mossy Creek Opens Annual Campmeeting August 9 For Week

Annual campmeeting will begin at historic Mossy Creek camp grounds, 18 miles north of Gainesville-Cleveland highway, on Monday, August 9, to continue through August 15.

Established 136 years ago, this is one of the oldest Methodist campmeetings in the section. Improvements on the grounds in recent years include a Memorial cottage in memory of the late Rev. C. B. McKenzie, which is occupied by the visiting ministers and singers.

A new swinging arbor, built in 1939, has electric lights, a large choir loft and excellent seating arrangements. The grounds have also been graded and set in Bermuda grass.

During the sessions this year, visiting preachers will include Rev. J. Foster Young, Gainesville District superintendent, Rev. R. J. Kerr, of Cedartown, Rev. F. E. Crutcher, Clayton, and Rev. D. L. Haygood. The singing will be led by Grady C. Looney, evangelistic song leader.

Life Saving Courses To Be Given Here By Red Cross

Plans are underway to organize classes for junior and senior Red Cross life saving, provided there are sufficient swimmers who want them, it is announced this week by Mrs. Agnes Wade, executive secretary of the local chapter.

Boys and girls from 12 to 16 years may enroll for the junior course which consists of 15 hours of instructions.

The senior course, open to swimmers over 17 years of age, carries 17 hours of instructions in all phases of life saving methods.

Those interested in taking either course are asked to telephone 467 and register immediately.

Red Cross Volunteers Are Needed

An increase in surgical dressing workers is greatly needed at the local Red Cross production rooms located upstairs in the Coca-Cola building on North Green street, it is announced this week by Mrs. Leslie F. Quinlan, Red Cross chairman of volunteer special service.

Although complete July reports have not been finished, the quota of 55,000 dressing is expected to fall short by at least 10,000, it was stated, and additional workers are urged to assist in making up at least 65,000 during the month of August.

The work room is open each morning of the week except Saturday and Sunday, from 9:30 to 12 o'clock. Special groups working at night include the Business and Professional Women's club and Pilot's club on Tuesday nights, members of the Service Men's Wives organization on Wednesday nights, and a group of Sunday

—Continued on Editorial Page

LUTHER REUNION

Mr. and Mrs. W. W. Luther, of Oakwood, well-known Hall countians, will jointly celebrate their 84th birthdays at a family reunion to be held at their home in Oakwood on Sunday, August 8. For many years the event has been the occasion for an annual gathering of friends and relatives of the couple.

In Florida

Corporal Clarence Scupin, Jr., son of Mr. and Mrs. Clarence Scupin, of 319 N. Bradford street, who is stationed at Drew Field, Fla., in the air and signal corps. He enlisted at Fort McPherson a year ago, received preliminary training at Walterboro, S. C., in camouflage work, going from there to Drew Field.

Farm Leaders Meet Here On August 11 To Hear Officials

Upwards of 150 farm leaders from Hall and surrounding counties are expected to attend an all day meeting here at the Hall county courthouse on Wednesday, August 11, when H. L. Wingate of Pelham, national director of the American farm bureau federation will be present.

Other officials of the organization expected to attend are R. G. Arnold, regional representative, and H. E. Woodruff, state organier. Each of 10 to 12 counties are expected to send around 15 of their outstanding farmers to the sessions.

H. G. Blackstock is president of the Hall county farm bureau.

Baptist Sunday School Convention To Meet Sunday Afternoon

The Chattahoochee Association Sunday school convention will meet Sunday afternoon at 3 o'clock at the First Baptist church. A fine program has been arranged with a godd speaker and special music, it is announced. All churches in the association are urged to send representatives and to bring reports.

Amendments Are Approved In Hall County

Hall county voters approved, by a vote of approximately four to one, the 28 amendments to the State constitution voted upon in Tuesday's election, thereby endorsing Governor Arnall's program of legislation as passed by the Legislature.

The amendment doing away with the so-called "pardon racket" received most favorable votes, while the one changing voting age from 21 to 18 years had most unfavorable votes registered against it.

Following is the vote:

No. 1—for 516; against 133.
No. 2—for 510; against 139.
No. 3—for 521; against 119.
No. 4—for 489; against 154.
No. 5—for 436; against 209.
No. 6—for 483; against 168.
No. 7—for 496; against 147.
No. 8—for 502; against 136.
No. 9—for 476; against 152.
No. 10—for 475; against 158.
No. 11—for 471; against 156.
No. 12—for 469; against 163.
No. 13—for 490; against 141.
No. 14—for 452; against 182.
No. 15—for 451; against 172.
No. 16—for 499; against 131.
No. 17—for 478; against 114.
No. 18—for 459; against 118.
No. 19—for 456; against 117.
No. 20—for 448; against 120.
No. 21—for 446; against 118.
No. 22—for 459; against 109.
No. 23—for 459; against 104.
No. 24—for 445; against 117.
No. 25—for 443; against 117.
No. 26—for 428; against 130.
No. 27—for 419; against 146.
No. 28—for 417; against 145.

Central Baptist W. M. S. To Begin Mission Study Course

All the circles of the Women's Missionary Society of Central Baptist church will meet at the church Monday, 2:30 p. m., for a mission study class, taught by Mrs. Will E. Bell, on the Indians.

All the women of the church are urged to come, and visitors will be welcome.

In Texas

Staff Sergeant Fred A. Crowe, son of Mr. and Mrs. H. C. Crowe of New Holland, who enlisted as a member of the military services in February 1941. At the present he is on duty with a medical corps that is stationed somewhere in Texas.

Tax Discounts Are Still Being Offered For Prompt Payment

Taxpayers in the city still can earn a discount on their local taxes by paying promptly, according to H. H. Pilgrim, clerk at the City Hall.

According to a schedule of graduated discounts in effect, property owners will be given a 1 per cent discount if taxes are paid in full by August 15, or a ½ per cent reduction if paid between August 16 and 31.

After that date the full amount will be due until October 8, after which tax penalties and interest will go into effect, it was stated.

The full discount of 2 per cent expired on July 15, and the 1½ per cent saving was effective through July 31.

"V for Victory" Is 35 Weeks Old

The Gainesville Eagle proudly presents for the 35th consecutive week its "V for Victory" feature, depicting Hall countians who have gone forth in answer to their country's call to conquer the enemies.

The Gainesville Eagle pledges to continue this honor to the country's service men and women through the cooperation of their friends and families on the home front.

The Gainesville Eagle wants you to bring by a photograph of your family member or special friend who has not yet appeared in this record of the contribution made by those brave and gallant men and women from Hall county in the magnificent accomplishments of the war effort.

All photographs are kept on file at The Eagle office for return to the owner, and the only charge in connection with publication is the cost of 90c to pay for having a newspaper cut made.

Co-Chairmen Added To War FinanceGroup

Announcement is made this week by J. H. Hosch, Hall county chairman of the War Finance committee, of the appointment of Rafe Banks and A. E. Roper as co-chairmen, to assist in formulating plans for the Third War Bond drive to begin in September. Judge A. C. Wheeler is honorary chariman also serving on the committee.

Other recent appointments are the new Treasury representatives including A. E. Willis, Chicopee manufacturing company, E. H. Ashley, Pacolet manufacturing company, C. E. Patterson, Owen-Osborne, and M. J. Green of Gainesville mills, whose activities will center especially on the purchase of War Bonds through payroll savings plans.

Latest reports from War Savings staff show that War Bond purchasers in Hall county bought a total of $37,181.25 in bonds and stamps in the period from July 1 through July 15, Mr. Hosch stated. The July quota for the county was $120,000.

REVIVAL SERVICES

Popular Springs church will begin its annual revival meeting on Saturday night, with services starting at 8:30 o'clock. The series will last through the week with services at night and also at 11 o'clock each morning. The pastor, Rev. Homer Morris, will preach.

SINGING

The Gainesville Mill church choir, extends to everyone a very special invitation to attend our regular monthly singing Sunday night, August 8, at the church.—H. W. Gittens, president.

In South Carolina

Harold DeLong, youngest son of Mr. and Mrs. Frank W. DeLong, who is now taking his basic training in the Navy Air corps at Columbia, S. C. He volunteered sometime ago for service, following the lead started by his oldest brother, now Major Frank DeLong, who recently returned from active service with the air corps in North Africa. His second brother, Second Lieutenant Jim DeLong, is now with an Army air corps unit somewhere in England.

Masons From 9th District Gather Here

Masons of the Ninth district will gather here Wednesday week, August 18, for the annual district convention. Upwards of 300 from the 80 lodges in the district are expected.

A number of officers from the Grand Lodge are scheduled to appear on the program, which is now being completed and which will be announced next week.

The convention is always a highlight in Masonic circles for the year in this section, with Gainesville lodge No. 219 acting as host and delegates on hand from practically all lodges. This is the largest district in the state in number of lodges and one of the largest in point of membership.

Wolf Addresses Three Civic Clubs On Post-War Plans

Speaking on the theme of post-war planning, H. Carl Wolf, Georgia chairman of the Committee of Economic Development, addressed a joint meeting of the three civic clubs—Rotary, Kiwanis and Lions—at the Dixie Hunt hotel Wednesday at the regular Kiwanis luncheon hour, with that club as host.

Wolf brought out that the American boys who are now marching on foreign battlefields are entering upon a new plane, and that

—Continued on Editorial Page

Truck Is Damaged In Wreck Friday

A heavy truck driven by Marston Thomas, and owned by the Jack Cole company, of Birmingham, was badly damaged Friday afternoon at New Holland when the load shifted after a defect developed in the rear spring, sending the machine into a telephone pole, according to records at State Patrol headquarters here. The pole was broken in two places, and an estimated $700 damage caused to the machine and its contents, consisting of airplane motors and parts, it was reported. The driver was not injured in the accident.

Overseas

Private James Elmo Crowe, who is a son of Mr. and Mrs. H. C. Crowe of New Holland. Private Crowe has been a member of his country's fighting forces since December, 1941. After completing his basic training in a coast artillery unit, he is now on duty overseas.

Successor Is Named To Charles S. Reid, Former Resident

Associate Justice R. C. Bell has been named by Governor Ellis Arnall to succeed Chief Justice Charles S. Reid, who recently tendered his resignation to enter military services, it is announced. Bell will be administered the oath of office on Friday morning at the state capitol.

The former Chief Justice is well-known in Gainesville, and was previously a resident here. At that time he served as cashier and vice-president of the Citizen bank, later entering the practice of law. His term was to have continued until January 1, 1947.

Rules Given For Overseas ChristmasMail

Army Postal Service announces that September 15 to October 15 will be "Christmas Mailing Month" for gifts to soldiers overseas, according to Lt. Colonel Hartley B. Dean, Chief of Postal Section, Headquarters Fourth Service Command.

Christmas packages must not be over five pounds in weight, 15 inches in length and 36 inches in length and girth combined. Packages must be packed tightly in metal, wooden or strong double-faced corrugated fiberboard boxes and should be marked "Christmas Gift Parcel." Only one package will be accepted during one week.

For Christmas packages mailing, restrictions are relaxed to make it unnecessary for the mailer to present either a request or an envelope bearing an APO cancellation

—Continued on Editorial Page

Roy Parks Resigns From Hall Selective Service Board Aug. 1

Roy Parks has resigned as a member of the Selective Service board of Hall county effective August 1, due to his health, it is announced. There will be no appointment to fill the vacancy at present. The other four board members will carry on the work of selecting men for service from the county, it is stated.

In North Africa

Corporal James E. Scupin, son of Mr. and Mrs. Clarence Scupin, of 319 N. Bradford street, who is now stationed in North Africa. He has been in service for 18 months, receiving his preliminary training at Fort Monmouth, N. J. He has been in foreign service for more than a year, in the signal corps.

Gainesville Officer Plays Active Part At Battle In Sicily

Lieutenant Bronson C. Glover, son of Mr. and Mrs. C. C. Glover of 847 E. Spring street is credited in recent news dispatches from Sicily with playing an important part as platoon leader in action that resulted in the capture of "Bloody Ridge," an almost perpendicular hill mass barring the American advance east along the northern coast near the village of San Stefano.

American officers who had been in North Africa said the taking of "Bloody Ridge" was comparable to the seizure of Hill 609 in Tunisia which paved the way for the capture of Mateur in the campaign there.

Twice the day before the capture of "Bloody Ridge" American troops had been beaten back by heavy Nazi fire, but the third time up their mission went on record as accomplished, the release reports.

REUNION POSTPONED

Plans for the annual Leckie-McCauley family reunion, which was to have been held August 8 at Hopewell Baptist church, have been called off for this year due to travel conditions, since relatives in South Carolina and parts of Georgia would be unable to attend. John F. Leckie, president.

Rev. E. H. Harrison Leaves for Chaplain School on Aug. 17

The Rev. Edward H. Harrison, priest in charge of the Grace Episcopal church, last Sunday received his orders to report to the Army Chaplain's school at Harvard university, and will leave on Auguest 17, it has been learned.

The Rev. Harrison had volunteered his services in the Spring of this year and will enter the army as first lieutenant.

He came to Gainesville to assume his duties at Grace church three years ago from Seabury Western seminary at Evanston, Ill., and during his stay has taken an outstanding part in the civic life of Gainesville, particularly in the leadership of young people of the community.

His successor at Grace church has not been named as yet.

In Alabama

Private First Class Thurston J. Henson, Jr., whose wife is the former Miss Sarah Stewart, daughter of Mr. and Mrs. C. H. Stewart of this city. He has been in the armed services since last January, is now stationed at Camp Sibert, Ala., where he is attached to a chemical warfare unit. His parents, Mr. and Mrs. T. J. Henson live in Montgomery, Ala.

Service Men Are Honored At Redwine

Soldiers and sailors of World War 2 are especially invited to meet with veterans of the Spanish-American war and World War I at the Redwine camp ground, six miles south of Gainesville, at their all day gathering on August 7, according to an announcement from H. Ewell Hope, chairman of the program, which starts at 10 a. m.

Every possible honor will be shown the men now in service, the sponsors announce. Several years ago when the ranks of the Confederates became thin, they asked that the Redwine reunion also include veterans of other wars. Thus the Spanish-American and World war veterans begain to meet at Redwine, and the purpose established to make this an annual meeting place for all veterans and their friends.

Highlighting the musical program planned for the day, the Army band from Camp Toccoa is expected to be present. The Mount Vernon and other quartets will also be scheduled on the program.

An array of speakers expected include Geo. B. Hamilton, state treasurer, Hammond Johnson, G. Fred Kelley, A. C. Wheeler, Jos. H. Blackshear, B. Frank Whelchel, E. D. Kenyon, Boyd Sloan, The Rev. Paul Smith, the Rev. C. E. Vaughan and many others, it is announced.

Although transportation problems are expected to keep those from great distances from attending, the sponsors expect thousands to at-

—Continued on Editorial Page

ANTIOCH MEETING

Tent holders at Antioch campgrounds are asked to meet on Tuesday, August 10, to assist in cleaning up the grounds in preperation for the annual campmeeting opening on August 17. In the event of rain on that day, they are asked to meet on the first fair day following, it is announced.

During the war, the *Gainesville Eagle* ran special issues highlighting men from Hall County serving in the military, placed in the shape of a "V" for victory. This front page also shows the extent to which war-related events and news dominated journalism of the time, in small cities as well as large.

Mack Abbott joined the Marine Corps in 1940, looking for adventure. Little did he know that he would be stationed at Pearl Harbor on December 7, 1941, to personally experience the "Day of Infamy." Surviving Pearl Harbor, he went on to serve in the 1st Marine Division, fighting on Guadalcanal and Pelilieu. These two photographs show the changes such fighting can make on a young man. At right, Abbott is pictured shortly after graduating from boot camp in 1940; below, two years later, he is on a transport ship headed to take part in another vicious landing on an enemy island.

Barney Burlson served in the Georgia National Guard before the war, parts of which were absorbed into the 30th Infantry Division once the war began. One of thousands of northeast Georgians to serve in the 30th from Normandy to Germany, Burlson returned home alive, though he had served in one of the most dangerous jobs imaginable, a combat infantryman. (Courtesy Hall County Library.)

Ed Jared, a pilot with the Army Air Forces, participated in one of the most remarkable theaters of the war, but one that has sadly received little attention. In an effort to assist Chinese allies, the United States made a commitment to supply them with as much war material as possible. The Japanese Navy made landing cargo ships on the coast impossible, so the only recourse was to supply them by air. This, however, meant flying over the largest mountain range in the world—the Himalayas. The danger was less from enemy aircraft than from the high altitude, long hours, and mountain peaks. Jared flew numerous missions over "the Hump" during the war and came back to work with Jesse Jewell to build northeast Georgia's poultry industry.

BRITISH EDITION

YANK
THE ARMY WEEKLY

3d SEPT. 5
1943
VOL. 2, NO. 12

By the men .. for the
men in the service

AFTER THE RAID

Marauder pilots discussing their
attack on France whose coast
they left less than half an hour
before this photo was taken.

Lt. Jim DeLong (left), gracing the cover of *Yank* magazine, served as a B-25 pilot in the European Theater. He flew over 100 missions over enemy territory, including two on D-Day in support of the allied landings.

Lloyd Smith, from Lula, enlisted in the US Army, was trained at Fort Benning, and was sent to Europe. Above, he is seen driving one of America's "wonder weapons," the Jeep, at Fort Benning. Below, after the hostilities have ended, he is part of the occupation forces in Germany with two of his friends.

Fran Johnson joined the Women's Army Corps (WACs), was trained as a clerk typist, and was sent overseas to serve as a secretary for an officer. Little did she know that the officer she would be assigned to was none other than Dwight D. Eisenhower, commander of all allied forces in Europe. She was a part of Eisenhower's staff from late 1944 until his recall from Europe after the German surrender in May 1945.

Desperate for a means to efficiently provide communications between loved ones at home and those serving overseas, V-mail was developed to alleviate the situation. Letters would be photographed and the film was shipped overseas, processed, and delivered. Pictured is an example to Hoke Moss's mother in Lula, a greeting from him and his Seabee battalion, a naval construction unit. The possibility of V-mail made drawn greetings as possible and as popular as written ones.

Richard Harris joined the Navy and became a pharmacist's mate. Harris was not aware at the time that many pharmacists' mates became medics for the Marine Corps, which is what happened to him. Though technically with the Navy, he found himself fighting alongside the Marines, being supplied with clothing and equipment from them. He is seen here armed with an M1 carbine rifle. Though medics (in the Marine Corps called "corpsmen") were not usually armed, the brutality of the Pacific battlefield made it an unfortunate necessity.

James Pierce of Gainesville joined the Army and was assigned to an artillery unit, serving with the occupation forces in the Philippines. When he returned home, his military training stood him in good stead, as he became a part of the police force.

Though not a veteran of World War II, Edgar Dunlap (above, center) had been an officer in France during World War I and had seen what war was like. In the years that followed, he became one of Hall County's greatest political leaders. It was in no small part thanks to him that federal funds were made available for rebuilding the city after the tornado. His influence and connections also convinced President Roosevelt (who had been his classmate at Harvard) to come in 1938 and to have the Navy locate the air station there in 1941.

Edgar Dunlap's son James was commissioned in the US Army as a cavalry officer, though by the 1940s that meant fast, light vehicles, not horses. He saw action in Europe against the Germans, served in the occupation forces, and came home to become a successful businessman, following in his father's footsteps.

The roughness of duty at the front is evidenced by this photograph of James Dunlap (right) somewhere in France, showing a strong contrast to the neatness and cleanliness in the previous photograph. Behind him is an armored M-2 Half Track vehicle used by cavalry units to scout ahead of the main forces and provide information back to command staff.

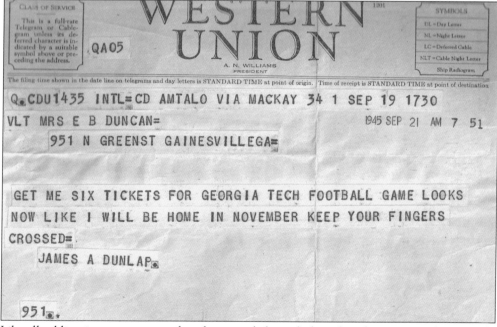

Like all soldiers in war, no matter how brave or dedicated, their thoughts turn ever homewards. As a graduate of Georgia Tech, James Dunlap was eager to attend a game as this telegraph shows. Sent to his family while still in Germany, he anticipates his homecoming with relish and a desire for things to return to "normal."

Occupation duty in Germany was not all dull, as James Dunlap discovered. At a victory celebration parade, he is close to the grandstand holding none other than Gen. George Patton (far left) and Gen. Georgi Zhukov (second to the left), the Soviet's most famous and capable general. Though tensions ran high between the erstwhile allies, these photographs seem to indicate that, for the moment at least, good relations were maintained.

Gainesville native John W. Jacobs Jr. (second from left) served as an artillery officer and a forward observer in the 30th Infantry Division. Fighting from Normandy to the Rhine, Jacobs saw much danger and was awarded two Silver Stars for his actions.

When the war ended, Jacob's previous journalism experience got him assigned to head up his unit's history in the war, the cover of which is shown here. After the war, Jacobs went on to become one of Hall County's leading businessmen, founding WDUN Radio, bringing cable television to the region, and eventually developing northeast Georgia's first internet news website.

Seven

VICTORY!

By 1945, the war was definitely going well for the United States and its allies. Two events in Hall County during the year not only helped give the final push to that victorious feeling, they also wisely addressed the postwar plans for Hall County and city of Gainesville. One was Harry Truman Day, a half-political, half-bond-raising effort on July 4, 1945, to show citizens of Gainesville the fruits of victory, the promise of the future, and also that a little more financial help was needed to assure such a victory. The victory parade in May was a celebration of all the efforts of those at home and in uniform and what they had finally—at great cost—achieved.

PRESIDENT HARRY S. TRUMAN DAY

INAUGURATING THE **POSTWAR DEVELOPMENT PROGRAM**

For a Greater Gainesville

JULY 4TH 1945

Gainesville, along with the rest of America, anticipated great prosperity with the end of the war. Here, a program for Harry Truman Day in 1945 presents Hall County's plan for new businesses, new residential areas, and new parks. Formulations were being made before final victory was even achieved. This is the front cover of the program for this momentous occasion.

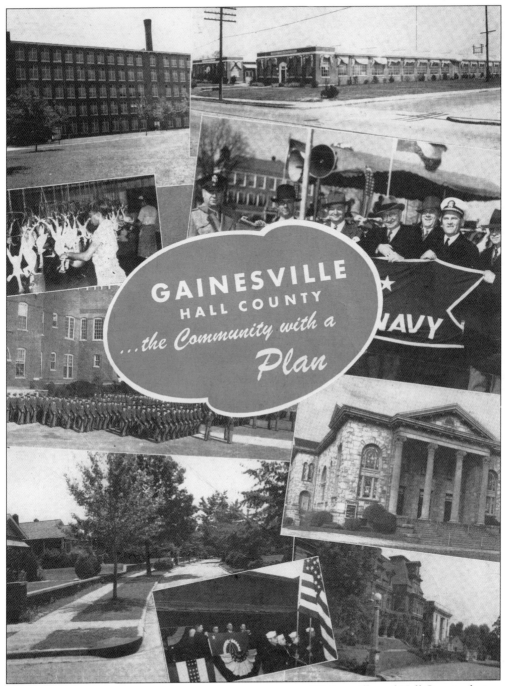

GAINESVILLE
HALL COUNTY
...the Community with a
Plan

The back cover of the program shows various scenes around Gainesville and Hall County during the war and highlights not only the county's contributions to the war effort, but the promise of prosperity to come.

Broad Street will be broadened from Chicopee to New Holland

New Golf Clubhouse to be built

New Professional Office Building to be erected

Green Street will be paved to Golf Club

New Memorial Building will house offices of Red Cross, American Legion and Chamber of Commerce

New Carver Homes will replace dwellings like this

New Armory will be erected at City Park

View typical of the 400 housing units for white people to be built in the Harry S. Truman Homes

Growth of infrastructure was considered one of the most important aspects of economic development in the postwar years, as this page from the program shows. Ghostly lines depict where the planned growth will take place and how it will look, including commercial as well as residential development. Unfortunately, it also gives signs that despite a war against the idea of racial superiority, segregation will be a part of the postwar world with separate housing for whites and blacks.

$3,925,000.00

FOR POSTWAR IMPROVEMENTS

In formulating our Harry S. Truman Development Program (the various projects of which are detailed below), we have tried to put first those improvements that are needed most—and that will contribute most to the health, happiness and general benefit of the people of Gainesville and Hall County.

If the supply of available labor and materials permits, some of those projects tentatively set up for 1948 and 1949 will be pushed forward to 1946 and 1947.

	DEVELOPMENT	COST	TO BE BEGUN
1	New Armory at City Park	$ 75,000.00	1945
2	New Water Works	150,000.00	1945
3	Broadening Broad Street from Chicopee to New Holland	100,000.00	1945
4	Extending Bradford Street to Thompson Bridge Road .	50,000.00	1946
5	Paving street from Green Street to Golf Club	25,000.00	1946
6	Building new Golf Club House (private funds) . . .	50,000.00	1946
7	New 20-unit Apartment House (private funds) . . .	100,000.00	1946
8	Harry S. Truman Homes—400 Units for White People (United States funds)	1,000,000.00	1945
9	Carver Homes—100 Units for Colored (U. S. funds) . .	500,000.00	1945
10	Memorial Building—Office of Red Cross, American Legion and Chamber of Commerce	300,000.00	1946
11	Improvement of Recreational Facilities	25,000.00	1945
12	New School Buildings	200,000.00	1946
13	Extension of Sewers and Water Mains, Disposal Plant .	100,000.00	1945
14	12 Miles New Paving	100,000.00	1946
15	Incinerator	50,000.00	1946
16	New Auditorium	100,000.00	1947
17	Public Library	75,000.00	1948
18	100-Bed Hospital (public and private funds)	500,000.00	1949
19	Construction of New Consolidated Bus Station on East Broad Street (corporate funds)	50,000.00	1946
20	New Freight Depot, Train Shed and Beautification of Grounds (corporate funds)	75,000.00	1947
21	Restoration of Cannon (from World War II) on Court House Square		
22	Installation of Automatic Dial Telephone System (corporate funds)	50,000.00	1947
23	Professional Office Building (corporate funds) . . .	250,000.00	1947

Total $3,925,000.00

This comprehensive development program of needed public works will assure Gainesville's freedom from unemployment in the critical re-conversion era.

The nuts and bolts of postwar planning for Hall County are shown in this preliminary budget. Practically no area was left unconsidered, including communications, transportation, water, and memorialization. Note also the short amount of time the plan was expected to take until completion: only four years at most.

Truman Day was an effort by Hall County leaders to not only show that they had a plan for the future, but to inspire one more big push for a war-bond drive. Shown is the main stand in front of the courthouse where newly appointed Postmaster General Hannagin, among other dignitaries, would deliver speeches to the crowd. A careful study of the image reveals that, again, the President Roosevelt podium is being used.

Here, organizers and participants of Truman Day pose for an official photograph. From left to right are Edgar Dunlap, Sen. Richard Russell, Rep. John S. Wood, Rep. Frank Boykin, Postmaster General Hannagin, and former Georgia governor Ed Rivers. Below, the dignitaries are underway, traveling to one of the whirlwind events scheduled for the single day.

Part of the bond-drive efforts on Truman Day included the Army Air Force's Shot from the Sky display and enemy aircraft whole and in parts. This display had already traveled all over the nation, and many citizens of Hall County turned out to see it. Pictured is a German BF-109 Messerschmitt fighter used to such devastating effect on the 8th Air Force's bombers over Europe.

In addition to the aircraft on display, all nearby members of the armed forces, including those from the naval school, the state guard, and Riverside Military Academy, held a parade. A Japanese Zero fighter can be seen in the foreground as the parade travels in front of the grandstand.

Another part of the day's festivities, and included in the parade here, was a series of horse-and-buggy races held just outside of town. Though urban compared to the rest of the region, horse transport was still very much a part of Hall County life, especially in terms of use in agriculture.

Participants in Hall County's VE Day (Victory in Europe) Parade are pictured lined up prior to marching. Members of the Navy (both male and female), Army students from Riverside, the Boy Scouts, the high school marching band, and civil defense volunteers can be seen. (Below, courtesy Hall County Library.)

In May 1945, Hall County celebrated VE Day by gathering on Roosevelt Square, where bands played, speeches were given, and military personnel from all over the state came to play a part in the parade that went up Main Street and wrapped around the square. Seen in the background is the courthouse, which was built in 1938 to replace the one that was destroyed by the tornado in 1936. (Courtesy Hall County Library.)

The parade makes its way down Main Street. At the front of the line are male personnel from the air station and naval school, while at the rear are two contingents of WAVES (Women Accepted For Volunteer Emergency Service). Over 200,000 women served in the US military during the war, almost 90,000 of them in the Navy. (Courtesy Hall County Library.)

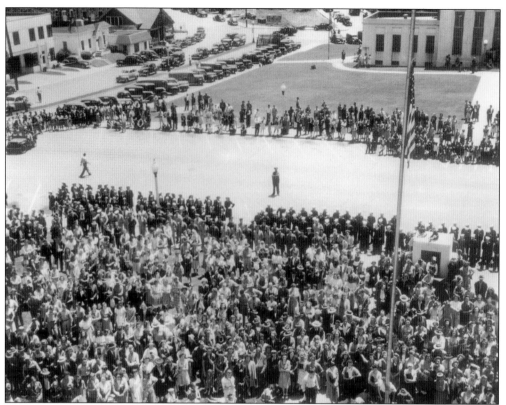

The parade has come to an end, marking not only a day of celebration, but also a sense of closure provided by community celebration of the defeat of one major enemy. Another was still active in the Pacific, but everyone knew it was only a matter of time. More lives would be lost before the end of battle in that theater in September 1945, but that victory positioned Hall County to take advantage of all possible avenues for advancement and growth in the years that followed the war. (Courtesy Hall County Library.)

Eight

THE POSTWAR BOOM

After the war, Hall County, much like the rest of the nation, emerged totally changed. Untouched by the devastation of the war, the country had experienced unprecedented growth and opportunity in just a short time. Many felt that the hope of future prosperity was one of the things that had been fought for, and so economic and social efforts were a peaceful continuation of the efforts that had been undertaken during the war years. With rationing over, the enemies defeated, the boys coming home, and the possibilities endless, it seemed that Hall County was poised on the brink of a renaissance. And so it was.

As the war was winding down, Hall County had changed from a rural county seat to a significant regional center of commerce, transportation, and communications. This ad, placed in the *Atlanta Journal*, was part of an effort by Hall County to highlight not only their efforts during the war, but also the prosperity that was sure to follow.

New roads and improvements of old ones were a major part of postwar planning. Here is a new road being cut in Murrayville, creating a way for the postwar boom in automobile use and production to reach its full potential. Yet, with the coming of the new, much of the old had to be sacrificed. Pictured in the background is the couple who owned this property and the house. They were most likely farmers, and their home and lives would be changed forever in the name of progress. (Courtesy Hall County Library.)

106

New roads for automobiles meant that older means of transportation, like trains, would take a backseat in the postwar world and lose their former dominance. These two photographs show the last run of a Gainesville & Midland Railroad engine, No. 209. The railroad had previously linked the city with points north and east, but lack of use and financial trouble finally spelled the end of it. The engine is still on display today behind the old depot in Gainesville. (Courtesy Hall County Library.)

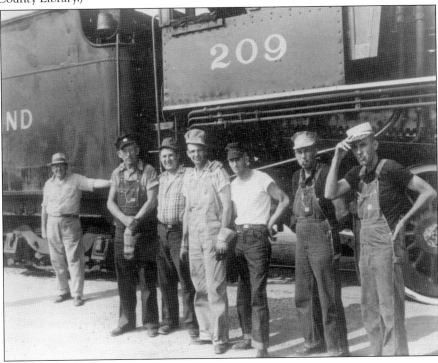

The square in the 1950s looked much as it had in the prewar years, but things were beginning to change. With new roads leading out of the city and new economic and industrial growth taking place away from the traditional town center, a decline was approaching that left the square a "figurehead" for ceremonies as businesses shut down or moved to where there was more traffic. (Courtesy Hall County Library.)

When John Jacobs Jr. returned after the war, he saw the need and potential for another radio station in Gainesville that would serve not just Hall County, but the entire northeast Georgia area. He and some partners created WDUN, which he eventually purchased to create one of Gainesville's most successful family businesses. Its success, and that of Jacobs, meant that he was one of the great civic leaders in postwar Hall County. (Courtesy Hall County Library.)

The largest postwar project for Hall County was the building of Buford Dam and the creation of Lake Sydney Lanier. The dam, shown during construction above and below, was built in neighboring Gwinnett County near Buford. Much of the filling and economic impact, however, would occur in Hall County. Construction began in 1950 and was completed in 1953, though achieving full pool required almost four more years.

The Navy, which had leased the field from Gainesville for $1 a year, turned ownership of it back over to the city. It became the major regional airport and was eventually named for Lee Gilmer, a local pioneer in flight. Many of the buildings were also put to use and became a technical school where veterans could study electronic technologies. One of those students was James Pierce, seated third from the left.

Opportunities increased for African American veterans thanks to the GI Bill. Here is a class of veterans at the Beulah Rucker School taking advantage of educational opportunities that had been impossible for them before the war. Beulah Rucker had been a champion of education for blacks since the early 20th century. (Courtesy Hall County Library.)

After its growth and success during World War II, Jesse Jewell, Inc. was poised to become one of the largest agricultural industries not just in Georgia, but in the entire Southeast. Leadership from Jewell and his company, which combined all aspects of poultry production from eggs to feed to packaging under one roof, made northeast Georgia the poultry capital of the world. The economic boom Hall County experienced after the war can be traced directly to this industry and the infrastructure and services created to serve it. This photograph shows the new Jewell plant around 1952, located close to the airport where Jewell operated a private aircraft.

So important had the poultry industry become that by 1950 Gainesville began holding an annual Poultry Parade accompanied by a festival atmosphere and the giving of awards. Here is the Jewell float for the parade in 1953. (Courtesy Hall County Library.)

Thanks to the Hill-Burton Act, significant funding became available for the building of medical facilities across the nation, and Hall County took full advantage of the opportunity. Seen here nearing completion is the new Hall County Hospital, a state-of-the-art facility with 90 beds. One fear, however, was that such a huge facility was inappropriate for the area. "We'll never fill that many beds," people were heard uttering. Rapid growth soon put those worries to rest, and Gainesville soon became one of the most respected medical communities in the entire state. (Courtesy Hall County Library.)

Shown is a 1949 aerial view of Gainesville. The city might have been physically transformed by the tornado of 1936, but the spirit arising out of that disaster gave it the strength to endure World War II. The county emerged from that war as a transportation, economic, social, and industrial powerhouse, with its citizens and veterans looking to the future. Though the changes that occurred in the postwar years might have eventually come to pass, there is no doubt that the experience of war accelerated and multiplied those changes, making Gainesville and Hall County the leading area in all of northeast Georgia.

Nine

HALL COUNTY TODAY

Since 1945, Gainesville has grown politically, culturally, economically, and socially. The Civil Rights Movement, spurred by the experiences of African Americans during the war, created a more equal society. Thanks to the poultry industry and the businesses created to support it, Hall County has had one of the highest per capita incomes in the nation. The resulting improvements in standard of living and affluence have meant resources are available to promote cultural institutions and pursuits that are unusual for communities of Gainesville's size. Though always looking to the future, Hall County has still taken time to remember its past and commemorate those who came before. The county's stature has led to significant influence in regional and state politics as well, and at the time of this writing both the governor and lieutenant governor are from Hall County.

Today, Gainesville and Hall County are still going strong and remain the center of commerce, transportation, culture, and influence for the entire northeast Georgia region. The roots of that success were sown in the trials of the 1930s and 1940s and, tended by visionary leaders and a community-wide spirit of cooperation, have created a harvest in the years since World War II that continue to benefit all generations, local and national.

An excellent view of Gainesville Square can be had today from the top level of the recently completed public parking deck. In recent years, revitalization efforts were developed to bring businesses and attractions back to the downtown area, and they have in large part succeeded. Though obscured by trees, "Old Joe" still gazes north, and the physical scars of the 1936 tornado have totally healed. The Jackson Building, from which the photographs on page 16 were taken, is on the far right.

New Holland Mills erected this monument in 1947 to honor its employees who had served in the military during the war. Over 500 employees served, and 17 were killed in action. The memorial can be seen today in front of the New Holland Mill building on Jesse Jewell Parkway.

This view from the old city hall building towards the courthouse shows how Roosevelt Square has changed since its dedication in 1938. Compare this image with those on pages 20 and 102. The roads that once surrounded and separated the two buildings and square have been removed or rerouted, making it accessible only by foot traffic.

This monument commemorates both of Franklin Delano Roosevelt's visits to Gainesville. One was two days after the tornado, and the second was two years later for the dedication of Roosevelt Square.

Dedicated in Roosevelt Square on Veterans Day, November 11, 1969, this monument pays tribute to all of Hall County's veterans from all wars. It is one of nearly 15 different monuments currently clustered in and around Roosevelt Square and Gainesville Square.

This view of the courthouse shows that while the landscaping might have changed, the building and monument have stood the test of time. Brass markers in the pavement in front of both buildings commemorate the WPA workers who built them between 1936 and 1938. Today, both buildings mostly house city and county offices.

The South Tower of Northeast Georgia Medical Center, previously Hall County Hospital, is pictured as it appears today. The 90 beds that "would never be filled up" have now grown to over 500, and the Medical Center is the single largest employer in the county. The original building is still there, but compare this image with that on page 113. The Medical Center is consistently ranked among the top hospitals in the state, and numerous other medical businesses and offices have grown up around the campus.

Engine No. 209 of the Gainesville Midland Railroad made the final trip of the line and was retired in 1969. It still sits where it came to rest and today is cared for by the City of Gainesville. It represents not only a bygone era, but it is a crucial reminder of what first made Gainesville the most important city in northeast Georgia.

Immediately after World War II, the poultry industry became dominant in the region and continues to be so today. Hall County is not only an industry leader in the state and nation, but worldwide. So important is the chicken in the county's history that this monument to it and the industry it supports was built in 1977. It stands today in "Poultry Park," across the road from Engine No. 209—a fitting junction of two of Hall County's most important histories.

Pictured is Brenau University today. Begun as a women's school, it soon became a college and is now a university, offering numerous graduate degrees, including a PhD in nursing.

After the war, the naval air station was given back to the City of Gainesville and renamed Lee Gilmer Airport. The amount of growth around the airport in this photograph from the 1990s is vastly apparent, especially when compared with that on page 46.

The most recent manifestation of the spirit of Hall County is the American Freedom Garden at the Northeast Georgia History Center. The brainchild of John Jacobs Jr., the garden serves not as a memorial but as a living testament to those who offered or gave their lives in service to their country. The bronze statue of five children at play, by artist Gary Price, allows visitors to join hands and complete the "circle of freedom."

BIBLIOGRAPHY

Abbott, Mack. *First and Last Shots Fired in World War II*. Fernandina Beach, FL: Wolfe Publishing, 2001.

Brice, W.M. *A City Laid Waste*. Self-published, 1936. Reprinted in Gainesville, GA: Georgia Printing Company, 1986.

Coughlin, Robert David. *Lake Sydney Lanier: A Storybook Site*. Atlanta: RDC Productions, 1998.

Hutchens, Linda Rucker and Ella J. Wilmont Smith. *Hall County, Georgia*. Charleston, SC: Arcadia Publishing, 2004.

Jacobs, John Jr. *The Longer You Live: Remembrances of John Wesley Jacobs, Jr*. Gainesville: Brenau University Press, 2009.

Jared, Edmond F. *One Hell of a Ride: A Memoir*. Athens, GA: Interviewyou, LLC, 2008.

Sawyer, Gordon. *Gainesville: 1900–2000*. Charleston, SC: Arcadia Publishing, 1999.

ABOUT THE ORGANIZATION

Glen Kyle, director of the Northeast Georgia History Center, is a native of north Georgia. Growing up in Blue Ridge, he graduated from North Georgia College in 1997 and has worked in museums since that time. Before coming to the Northeast Georgia History Center, he served as exhibits manager and then as curator of military history at the Atlanta History Center, as well as having served on the board of the Georgia Association of Museums and Galleries. His personal interests lie in the areas of military and medieval history, and he received his MA in history from North Georgia College and State University in 2012. He lives in Dacula, Georgia, with his wife, Priscilla, and their two sons, Brendan and Andrew.

This work was completed primarily as a product of the Northeast Georgia History Center and its archival collections. The Northeast Georgia History Center, born as the Georgia Mountains Museum, resided for many years in the Green Street Fire House in Gainesville. It moved to its current home in 2004, a 26,000-square-foot facility on the Brenau University campus. Our vibrant, growing, and professional institution now reaches out to a 13-county area. The White Path Cabin, Land of Promise, Mark Trail, Northeast Georgia Pottery exhibits, and educational programming make the history center one of the best destinations in the region for learning about the life and times of those who came before us. The American Freedom Garden helps us honor those who preserve the gift of freedom.

For more information, please visit the Northeast Georgia History Center's website at www.negahc.org.

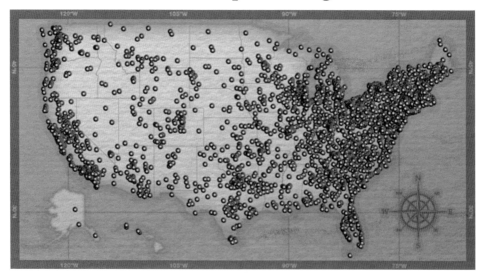